MORTGAGE PROCESSING MADE EASY

by Mr. Min

Table of Contents

To Readers of This Book

Thank you so much for choosing this book as your choice.

I've been in mortgage industry for more than 25 years and saw lot of people making enough money to live in comfortable and luxurious life style.

I have both retail and wholesale working as loan originator, processor, underwriter, 2ndary and program production.

As I prepare for my retirement, I wanted to help newcomers to get in to the mortgage industry little bit easier.

It is a very rewarding industry but it is not easy to get in.

There are some books but don't explain actual task nor details.

I hope this book will teach basics of mortgage to people who wants to be loan agent and processor.

Guidelines change very often but once you know and understand the basic concept of guidelines it should be easy to adapt changes.

Just remember couple of things.

1. Do not assume anything
2. Apply basic common sense
3. Be professional
4. You are helping borrowers not scheming

Sounds easy but not lot of people remember when it comes down to money.

Website is on the way for more information and FAQs. Please email your contact information to hellomrmin123@gmail.com for newsletter and updates.

Mr. Min

8/24/2022

Chapter 1.
THE PROCESSOR

What is mortgage processor

Processor's main job is to gather borrower's documents through LO (Loan Originator) and package a submission file for the lender, submit and follow up until close of escrow.

As a processor, you will be the main communicator between LO and the lender.

There are several types of processing. We will be talking about the most common and important type of processing.

Processing from start to end. You will need knowledge on the mortgage industry, loan products, compliances, guidelines, and more.

Once you have all around knowledge of residential mortgage, it will be a very rewarding job for anyone who wants everyday challenges with fast moving exciting industry.

Processors must have to have good communication skills. You are the communicator between the loan originator and the lender.

This book is based on Fannie Mae products which are the most commonly used programs.

There are two types of states for the mortgage. Wet and Dry states.

Wet states use lawyers and dry states use escrow for closing agents.

California is a dry state and we will use California's law on this book.

Some states like Texas have restrictions on guidelines but most states use the same guidelines.

What makes a good processor

A good processor is a person who closes the loans on time with less hassle.

Communication between LOs and lenders are very important.

Each person has different ways of follow ups, organize files.

You need to make sure you know how many files and documents for each file are needed.

You must be aware of the status of each file.

As a processor, you would like to know the full scenario and details of the loan to structure it.

You can't structure the loan without a full list of documents for the loan product.

Here's the most important things you must remember.

- Make sure to have plans for the stress build up.
- **Must gather all documents before structuring the loan.**
- **Do NOT submit a loan when you don't have all information even if you don't have enough time to close the loan. Can't change the loan scenario after submitting.**
- **Must review and verify documents before submitting to the lender.**
- **Think like an underwriter and think ahead of conditions.**

- If additional documents are requested by the lender, DO NOT PIECEMEAL. Underwriter DOES NOT remember your file. Underwriter doesn't want to review the file each time you send conditions in.
- It is always better to send all conditions at once.
- Good relationships with A/E, A/M and underwriters are very important.
- Review all documents before contacting the borrower and ask for additional documents and answers for the questions at the same time.

***Underwriters don't want to review files several times. They can't remember all the details of the loan.**

If you send in conditions piece by piece, they have to review again and again.

Underwriters will hate you and give you a hard time closing all of your loans.

What do you do as a processor

Processor's job is not that hard once you make your own routine.

Mostly you gather documents, review documents, verify documents and communicate.

Processors need to know:

- Documents to review and verity
    - o Income
    - o Asset
    - o RPA
    - o Credit report
    - o Title report

  - Escrow instruction
  - Insurance coverage
  - HOA questionnaire
  - Fannie Mae forms
- Must to know guidelines for the loan products
- Fannie Mae guideline is a must
- How to structure a loan
- How to read the rate sheet
- Mortgage forms
- Mortgage terms

Each company has their own ways of procedure.

There are three most commonly used ways but you must know all processor's tasks.

1. You do most of work, you make most money with this kind of practice

Usually, LO will contact the borrower and get all the documents before bringing the file to the processor but for some companies LO will get a loan application and ask the processor to find the loan product and necessary document list with the loan scenario.

Processor packages the loan and submits it to the lender.

2. Plain processing

LO will contact the borrower, get a loan application, documents and select a loan program.

You just package it and submit it to the lender.

3. Less work, less money

This practice is largely used by banks, credit unions and large size mortgage lenders.

LO will do most of the processing up to packaging and will submit it to the underwriter for an approval.

Underwriter will underwrite the file and approve the loan with conditions and conditions will be sent to the processor.

Processor gets the file for the first time and follows up with LO.

As a processor, you must know what documents are required, how to review documents, packaging, and follow up with the lender.

What will you learn

You don't need to have any experience on mortgage for this book. You just need to understand the basic concept of mortgage underwriting.

Why do I need to learn the underwriting concept? Well, you are packaging a loan file for the underwriter. It is very important to understand and know what underwriters are looking for in a loan package.

Career path of the processor

Most likely you will start out as an assistant of a senior processor. You will need to learn how to package and review documents to become a processor.

Lot of senior processors get a job as underwriter to improve their career.

Chapter 2.
BEFORE WE BEGIN

What is mortgage (home loan)

- Residential mortgage is used for 1 to 4 units.
- 5 units and more are considered commercial properties and can't be done with residential mortgages.

Terms you must know

DU : Automated underwriting system for Fannie Mae

LP : Automated underwriting system for Freddie Mac

LOS : Loan origination system (software)

LO : Loan Originator (Loan agent, loan officer)

Escrow officer : Closing agent

1003 : Loan application

1008 : Loan summary by 1003

PITI : **P**rincipal, **I**nterest, Property **T**ax, Property **I**nsurance (P+I = mtg. payment)

LTV : Loan To Value (Loan amount ÷ Purchase price or Appraised Value whichever less)

DTI : Debt to Income (total expenses ÷ gross income)

PTD : Prior to Doc (prior to loan doc) conditions

PTF : Prior to Funding conditions

CTD : Clear to DOC

CTC : Clear to close

EOI : Evidence of insurance

Loss pay clause : An insurance contract endorsement where an insurer pays a third party for a loss instead of the named insured or beneficiary

4506 : IRS form to request for transcript of tax return

HOA cert. : Same as "HOA questionnaire", "Condo Cert." for condo, PUD projects

RPA : Residential Purchase Agreement

Listing agent : Real estate agent for the SELLER

Selling agent : Real estate agent for the BUYER

Credit supplement : Updated information on a credit report

EMD : Same as " Initial deposit", "Earnest money deposit"

Prelim : Preliminary title report, same as "Title report"

SSA - 89 : Social Security Administration form to verify social security number

Borrower Cert. : Borrowers' Certification and Authorization form

COC : Changed Circumstance Form is used if there's changes in rate, terms, etc.

Fee Sheet : Form to show list of itemized fees

Rate sheet : Rate sheet shows daily pricing for the mortgage products

Add-ons : Fees related to each scenario

Lock request : Locking interest rate

DOC request : Requesting loan doc after locking a loan

Funding : Wiring final funds from lender

Recording : Recording finalizes the transaction legally to subject county

Margin : Margin on the rate

Index : Index to determine the interest rate

Teaser rate : Initial rate agreed on the terms of the note

Ceiling : Highest interest rate that can go up to

Floor : Lowest interest rate that can go down to

Caps : Maximum interest rate can be increased by the terms of the note

VOE : Verification of Employment form showing itemized income

VOD : Verification of Deposit form

VOR : Verification of Rent or Mortgage form for housing history

Gift letter : Letter from donor for gift funds for the borrower

Gift : Gift funds for the borrower without obligation of paying back

LOE : Letter of explanation

Contingency : Purchase transactions have contingency dates for inspection and loan

Appraisal report : Evaluation report of the subject property

Rental survey : Market rental amount evaluation

PIW : Property Inspection Waiver (if DU approved PIW, appraisal <u>MUST NOT be ordered</u>)

Trade line : Borrower's record of activity for any type of credit extension reported to a credit reporting agency

Non-traditional credit : Record of activities not reported in credit report such as utilities

Vesting : Details of the actual ownership of property

Basic math

DTI (Debt to Income Ratio)

When you look at the loan summary sheet (1008) and / or loan approval sheet, you will notice '/' between two numbers on the DTI section like 39/43.

They are called front DTI and Back DTI.

- Front DTI: Only counts payments for the subject loan to calculate DTI
- Back DTI: Includes all payments to calculate DTI

***What is included in payment calculation for the DTI**

- Subject property
  - Loan payment amount
  - All property tax
  - Home insurance (includes HO6 if applicable. HO6: wall to wall coverage for attached homes)
  - HOA dues (if applicable)
- Other payments
  - Installment payment 10 or more number of payments left
  - Leased automobile regardless of number of payments
  - Revolving accounts
  - Student loans (deferred or not)

***What is NOT included in payment calculation for the DTI**

- Installment payments that have 10 or less payments
- Personal insurances like life, health and automobile, etc.
- Personal utilities like water, power, phone, etc.
- Business related payments that are paid by the business

- Payments made by 3rd party for at least 12 months currently

Example

Borrower:

- Income $10,000
- Payments on credit report $1,000

Subject property payments

- Mortgage payment $1,500
- Property tax $800
- Home insurance $200

Total house expense $2,500

Total expense = total house expense + total payments on credit report

$2,500 + $1,000 = $3,500

Front DTI = Subject property payments / Income

$2,500 / $10,000 = 25%

Back DTI = Total expense / Income

$3,500 / $10,000 = 35%

You write 25/35 for DTI

LTV, CLTV, HCLTV

- LTV: Loan to Value
- CLTV: Combined Loan to Value
- HCLTV: Home Equity Combined Loan to Value (when there's a HELOC)

When processing a loan, LTV is always the loan you are working on.

If you are working on a 1st lien, calculate LTV with a 1st loan amount.

If you are working on a 2nd lien, calculate LTV with a 2nd lien loan amount.

Example a

Purchase price: $500,000

Appraised value: $500,000

Down payment: $100,000

1st Loan amount: $400,000

LTV: 1st loan (400,000) / purchase price (500,000) = 80%

CLTV: no 2nd lien. CLTV is same as LTV

Example b

Purchase price: $500,000

Appraised value: $500,000

Down payment: $100,000

1st Loan amount: $400,000

2nd Loan amount: $50,000

LTV: 1st loan (400,000) / purchase price (500,000) = 80%

CLTV: 2nd loan (50,000) / purchase price (500,000) = 10%

1st lien (80%) + 2nd lien (10%) = CLTV is 90%

Example c

Purchase price: $500,000

Appraised value: $480,000

Down payment: $100,000

1st Loan amount: $400,000

LTV: 1st loan (400,000) / appraised value (480,000) = 83.34%

*** always calculate LTV with 'purchase price' or 'appraised value' whichever less.**

CLTV: no 2nd lien. CLTV is same as LTV

Loan flow

1. Application from the borrower
2. Gather documents from borrowers
3. Review and verify all documents
4. Packing
5. Submit file to a lender
6. Loan approval from the lender
7. Provide additional documents requested from the lender
8. Lock interest rate
9. Order loan doc
10. Borrower signs the loan doc
11. Funding & recording
12. Congratulations, the loan is closed!

Chapter 3.
MORTGAGE LOAN BASIC

What makes a TRID loan application

After receiving a loan application, initial disclosure must be sent to the borrower within 3 business days per compliance. *Very important.

TRID loan application triggers the disclosure requirements.

If the borrower didn't provide all 6 items listed below, LO doesn't need to send out disclosures.

TRID (TILA-RESPA integrated disclosures) is also known as the Know Before You Owe mortgage disclosure.

The Consumer Financial Protection Bureau implemented TRID to inform and protect consumers when applying for real estate mortgages.

6 pieces of information are needed to be considered an application that triggers the requirement for disclosure.

1. Name
2. Income
3. Social Security Number

4. Property Address
5. Estimated Value of the Subject Property
6. Mortgage Loan Amount Wanted

What makes 1st, 2nd, etc. lien

A property lien is **a legal claim on assets that allows the holder to obtain access to the property if debts are not paid.**

Recording date determines the position of the lien. **Position of the lien determines who gets paid first. 1st position lien has priority rights.**

Earliest recorded lien is the 1st TD (Trust Deed), 2nd earliest recorded lien is 2nd TD and so on.

Subordinate Loans

Loans other than 1st TD.

Unacceptable Subordinate Financing Terms

- Mortgage with negative amortization
- Subordinate financing that does not fully amortize under a level monthly payment plan where the maturity or balloon payment date is less than five years after the note date of the new first mortgage

Eligible Variable Payment Terms for Subordinate Financing

- Monthly payment must remain constant for each 12 months period over the term of the subordinate lien mortgage
- Monthly payments for all subordinate liens must cover at least the interest due so that negative amortization does not occur

Companies involved in transaction

Purchase transaction

Company	What do they do
Real Estate Brokerage / agent	Represents buyer and / or seller
Escrow / Closing agent	Calculate and disburse as a 3rd party
Title	Manage legality
Loan Lender / Broker / agent	Packaging loan / Lending money

Refinance transaction

Company	What do they do
Escrow / Closing agent	Calculate and disburse as a 3rd party
Title	Manage legality
Loan Lender / Broker / agent	Packaging loan / Lending money

Loan Types

Conventional

Conforming and high-balance loan limits are set yearly.

- Conforming: Loan limits are same for all states and counties
- High-Balance:
  - o Loan amount greater than conforming amount up to high-balance limit
  - o Loan limits are set by the states and county

Fannie Mae Loan Limits for 2022

	Conforming Limits	High-Balance *
1 unit	$647,200	$970,800
2 units	$828,700	$1.243.050
3 units	$1,001,650	$1,502,475
4 units	$1,244,850	$1,867,275

Government

- FHA: 3.5% down is required. Better pricing than conventional
- VA: 100% financing is available

Jumbo

Any amount over conventional limits is considered as Jumbo

Non-QM (Non-Qualified Mortgage)

Non-QM loans are used for the loans that are not qualified for conventional loans.

A significant difference between a QM loan and a Non-QM is that a Non-QM loan uses alternative methods of income verification.

All conventional and government products are QM loans.

Loan Purpose (Transaction Types)

Purchase

Purchase transactions for 1 to 4 units.

Rate & Term Refinance (Limited cash-out)

- Rate & term refinance must have benefits to the borrower such as lower interest rate, lower monthly payments, etc.
- Cash-back to borrower $2,000 or 2% of the loan amount, whichever less.

Acceptable transactions

- Modifying the interest rate and/or term for existing mortgages
- Paying off the unpaid principal balance of the existing first mortgage including prepayment penalties
- From construction loan to permanent loan

- Receiving cash back less of 2% of the new loan amount or $2,000
- Buying out a co-owner pursuant to an agreement
- Paying off a subordinate mortgage lien used to purchase the subject property
- Paying off the unpaid principal balance of PACE loans and other debt used for energy related improvements

Ineligible transactions

- Property tax is included in the new loan and escrow account is not set up
- More than 60 days delinquent property tax is included in the new loan
- Paying off non-purchase 2nd TD
- Any refinance with refinanced history within last 6 month

Cash-out Refinance

Transactions must meet the following requirements

- Transaction must be used to pay off existing mortgages by obtaining a new first mortgage secured by the same property or be a new mortgage on a property that does not have a mortgage lien against it
- Properties that were listed for sale must have been taken off the market on or before the disbursement date of the new mortgage
- The property MUST have been purchased by the borrower at least SIX months prior to the disbursement date of the new mortgage except for the following:
  - o No waiting period if the borrower acquired the property through an inheritance or was legally awarded the property (divorce, separation, or dissolution of a domestic partnership)
  - o The delayed financing requirements are met.

- If the DTI ratio exceeds 45%, six months reserves is required by DU

Ineligible Transactions

- The mortgage loan is subject to a temporary interest rate buydown
- The subject property was purchased by the borrower within the six months preceding the disbursement date of the new mortgage
- The borrower who refinances the first mortgage loan and have sufficient equity to pay off the PACE loan but choose not to do so will be ineligible for a cash-out refinance
- Transactions in which a portion of the proceeds of the refinance is used to pay off the outstanding balance on an installment land contract, regardless of the date the installment land contract was executed
- The new loan amount includes the financing of real estate taxes that are more than 60 days delinquent and an escrow account is not established, unless requiring an escrow account is not permitted by applicable law or regulation

Delayed Financing Exception

- The original purchase transaction was an arms-length transaction
- The borrower may have initially purchased the property as one of the following:
  - A natural person
  - An eligible inter vivos revocable trust
  - A LLC or partnership in which the borrower has an individual or joint ownership of 100%

- o The original purchase transaction has no mortgage financing was used to obtain the subject property - The preliminary title search or report must confirm that there are no existing liens on the subject property
- o The new loan amount can be no more than the actual documented amount of the borrower's initial investment in purchasing plus the financing of closing costs, prepaid fees, and points on the new mortgage loan

Occupancy

Primary / Owner Occupied

- Borrower is occupying the subject property
- Multiple borrowers: Only one borrower must occupy and take title to the property.

Military service members: A military service member borrower currently on active duty and temporarily absent from their principal residence. Must obtain a copy of the borrower's military orders.

- Parents or legal guardians wanting to provide housing for their handicapped or disabled adult child: If the child is unable to work or does not have sufficient income to qualify for a mortgage on their own.
- Children wanting to provide housing for parents: If the parent is unable to work or does not have sufficient income to qualify for a mortgage on their own.

2nd Home / Vacation home

- Must be occupied by the borrower for some portion of the year
- Is restricted to one-unit dwellings
- Must be suitable for year-round occupancy

- The borrower must have exclusive control over the property
- Must not be rental property or a timeshare arrangement
- Cannot be subject to any agreements that give a management firm control over the occupancy of the property
- DU only, no manual underwriting is allowed

Investment / Non-owner Occupied

An investment property is owned but not occupied by the borrower.

Property Types

Detached / Attached :

- Detached property does not share any walls with other property
- Attached property shares at least one wall with other property

Types

- SFR (Single Family Residence)
- Condo (Low rise & High rise)
- PUD (Planned Unit Property)
- 2 to 4 units (multiple units in one parcel)

Escrow account (Impound account)

Mortgage payment includes loan principal and loan interests.

Borrower usually pays property tax and hazard insurance (home insurance) separately, however the borrower has the option to pay property tax and / or hazard insurance with mortgage payments by setting up an escrow account.

DOC Types

DOC type can be described as a way of verifying income and assets of the borrower.

Full DOC has the best pricing.

DOC Types	Income docs	Asset docs	Employment
Full Doc	Yes	Yes	Yes
Alt Doc (VOE, P&L, etc.)	Yes	Yes	Yes
SIVA	Stated - no docs	Yes	Yes
SISA	Stated - no docs	Stated - No docs	Yes
NINA			
No Doc	No	No	No

Document requirements for DOC type

***All documents have to be most recent.**

** **Document requirements are vary by the loan product**

DOC Types	Income docs	
	Wage Earners	Self-employed
Full Doc	• 2 yrs W-2s • Pay stubs to cover 1 full month	• 2 yrs tax returns for business & personal
Alt Doc	• VOE form • 12 months bank statements	• P & L statement • 12 months bank statements
SIVA	N/A	N/A
SISA	N/A	N/A
No Doc	Leave blank	Leave blank

DOC Types	Asset docs	
	Wage Earners	Self-employed
Full Doc	• 2 months bank statements	• 3 months business bank statements • 2 months personal bank statements
Alt Doc	• 2 months bank statements	• 3 months business bank statements • 2 months personal bank statements
SIVA	• 2 months bank statements	• 3 months business bank statements • 2 months personal bank statements
SISA	N/A	N/A
No Doc	Leave blank	Leave blank

Term Types

- Fixed: Monthly payment is fixed for the life of the loan
- ARM: Interest rate is fixed for teaser period and changes by the terms of the note
    - 5/1 ARM: Teaser rate is fixed for 5 years with annual recast
    - Teaser rate = Locked rate = Starting rate
    - Interest rate = Index + Margin after teaser rate
    - 5/2/5: 1st adjust cap / Annual cap / Ceiling
- I/O: Make interest only payments for the agreed period by the terms of the note
- HELOC: Usually used for 2nd TD and payments are based on principal balance

Compensation Plan

Compensation plans are how LO gets paid.

Lender Paid

Pricing is negotiated between the broker and the lender.

When "lender paid" compensation is selected, you may not receive compensation or fees from the borrower.

Borrower Paid

Origination and processing fees will be paid directly by the borrower.

Broker compensation will not be added in the pricing.

Mortgage interest rate vs APR

APR (annual percentage rate) reflects the mortgage interest rate PLUS other charges.

There are many costs associated with taking out a mortgage. Includes:

- The interest rate
- Points
- Fees
- Other charges

The interest rate is the cost you will pay each year to borrow the money, expressed as a percentage rate. It does not reflect fees or any other charges you may have to pay for the loan.

An annual percentage rate (APR) is a broader measure of the cost of borrowing money than the interest rate. The APR reflects the interest rate, any points, mortgage broker fees, and other charges that you pay to get the loan. For that reason, your APR is usually higher than your interest rate.

What are (discount) points and lender credits and how do they work

Generally, points and lender credits let you make tradeoffs in how you pay for your mortgage and closing costs. Points, also known as discount points, lower your interest rate in exchange paying for an upfront fee. Lender credits lower your closing costs in exchange for accepting a higher interest rate.

These terms can sometimes be used to mean other things. "Points" is a term that mortgage lenders have used for many years. Some lenders may use the word "points" to refer to any upfront fee that is calculated as a percentage of your loan amount, whether or not you receive a lower interest rate. Some lenders may also offer lender credits that are unconnected to the interest rate you pay – for example, as a temporary offer, or to compensate for a problem.

The information below refers to points and lender credits that are connected to your interest rate. If you're considering paying points or receiving lender credits, always ask lenders to clarify what the impact on your interest rate will be.

Points

Points let you make a tradeoff between your upfront costs and your monthly payment. By paying points, you pay more upfront, but you receive a lower interest rate and therefore pay less over time. Points can be a good choice for someone who knows they will keep the loan for a long time.

Points are calculated in relation to the loan amount. Each point equals one percent of the loan amount. For example, one point on a $100,000 loan would be one percent of the loan amount, or $1,000. Two points would be two percent of the loan amount, or $2,000. Points don't have to be round numbers – you can pay 1.375 points ($1,375), 0.5 points ($500) or even 0.125 points ($125). The points are paid at closing and increase your closing costs.

Paying points lowers your interest rate relative to the interest rate you could get with a zero-point loan at the same lender. A loan with one point should have a lower interest rate than a loan with zero points, assuming both loans are offered by the same lender and are the same kind of loan. For example, the loans are both fixed-rate or both adjustable-rate, and they both have the same loan term, loan type, same down payment amount, etc. The same kind of loan with the same lender with two points should have an even lower interest rate than a loan with one point.

Points are listed on your Loan Estimate and on your Closing Disclosure on page 2, Section A. By law, points listed on your Loan Estimate and on your Closing Disclosure must be connected to a discounted interest rate.

The exact amount that your interest rate is reduced depends on the specific lender, the kind of loan, and the overall mortgage market. Sometimes you may receive a relatively large reduction in your interest rate for each point paid. Other times, the reduction in interest rate for each point paid may be smaller. It depends on the specific lender, the kind of loan, and market conditions.

It's also important to understand that a loan with one point at one lender may or may not have a lower interest rate than the same kind of loan with zero points at a different lender. Each lender has their own pricing structure, and some lenders may be more or less expensive overall than other lenders – regardless of whether you're paying points or not. That's why it pays to shop around for your mortgage. Explore current interest rates or learn more about how to shop for a mortgage.

Lender credits

Lender credits work the same way as points, but in reverse. You pay a higher interest rate and the lender gives you money to offset your closing costs. When you receive lender credits, you pay less upfront, but you pay more over time with the higher interest rate.

Lender credits are calculated the same way as points, and may appear on lenders' worksheets as negative points. For example, a lender credit of $1,000 on a $100,000 loan might be described as negative one point (because $1,000 is one percent of $100,000).

That $1,000 will appear as a negative number as part of the Lender Credits line item on page 2, Section J of your Loan Estimate or Closing Disclosure. The lender credit offsets your closing costs and lowers the amount you have to pay at closing.

In exchange for the lender credit, you will pay a higher interest rate than what you would have received with the same lender, for the same kind of loan, without lender credits. The more lender credits you receive, the higher your rate will be.

The exact increase in your interest rate depends on the specific lender, the kind of loan, and the overall mortgage market. Sometimes, you may receive a relatively large lender credit for each 0.125% increase in your interest rate paid. Other times, the lender credit you receive per 0.125% increase in your interest rate may be smaller.

A loan with a one-percent lender credit at one lender may or may not have a higher interest rate than the same kind of loan with no lender credits at a different lender. Each lender has their own pricing structure, and some lenders may be more or less expensive overall than other lenders – regardless of whether or not you're receiving lender credits. Explore current interest rates or learn more about how to shop for a mortgage.

See an example

The chart below shows an example of the tradeoffs you can make with points and credits. In the example, you borrow $180,000 and qualify for a 30-year fixed-rate loan at an interest rate of 5.0% with zero points. In the first column, you choose to pay points to reduce your rate. In the third column, you choose to receive lender credits to reduce your closing costs. In the middle column, you do neither.

Compare 3 scenarios of how points affect interest rate

Rate	4.875%	5.000%	5.125%
Points	**+0.25**	**0**	**-0.25**
Borrower's situation	Borrower plans to keep mortgage for a long time. Borrowers can afford to pay more cash at closing.	Borrower is satisfied with the market rate without points in either direction.	Borrower doesn't want to pay a lot of cash up front.
Borrower may choose	Pay points now and get a lower interest rate.	Zero points.	Pay a higher interest rate and get a lender credit toward some or all of closing costs.
What that means	Borrowers might agree to pay more in closing costs, in exchange for a lower rate and make less monthly payments.	With no adjustments in either direction, it is easier to understand what to pay and to compare prices.	Borrower might agree to a higher rate in exchange for lender's credit toward closing costs.

Fees and charges

When you are buying a home you generally pay all of the costs associated with that transaction. However, depending on the contract or state law, the seller may end up paying for some of these costs.

Even if you don't pay the mortgage closing fees directly out of pocket, you might end up paying them indirectly. Sometimes, you can negotiate with the seller for a "credit" towards your closing costs, but the seller will usually require you to pay a higher price for the home in order to cover the costs of this credit.

You're still paying for these costs. They are just paid through your loan instead of paid out of pocket. The lender may also offer to give you a credit to help with your closing costs. This credit isn't free either. Typically, the lender will either increase your loan amount to cover these costs, or charge you a higher interest rate in exchange for the credit.

Common closing fees or charges may include:

- Appraisal fees
- Tax service provider fees
- Lender fees
- Origination fees
- Title insurance
- Escrow fees
- Government taxes
- Prepaid expenses such as property taxes, property insurance, HOA dues and interest until your first payment is due

Compliance

What makes compliance so important?

Compliances are there to protect the borrowers.

Following compliance procedures are the most important in mortgage transactions.

Dates, fees and timely sent disclosures to borrowers are very very very important.

Required license to originate mortgage

- individual MLO license DFPI
- active DRE broker & MLO endorsement
- DRE sales & MLO endorsement
- CFL license through an individual
- CFL (California Financing Law)
- CFL license can only originate through CFL lenders

- Employee, processor, underwriter does not require any license
- Contract underwriter, processor need license

Section 32 (High Cost Loans)

- Applies to purchase, refinance, and HELOC
- Mortgage Insurance (MI) is not included as fee
- bona fide discount point: rate buy-down fee is not included as fee

It becomes high-cost loan when APR is higher than APOR on Lock date

- 1st mortgage: 6.5%
- 1st mortgage with loan amount less than $50,000 : 8.5%
- 2nd mortgage: 8.5%

Maximum Origination Fees for 1st mortgage

- 5% of the total loan amount for a loan of $22,969 or more
- The lesser of 8% or $1,148 of the total loan amount for a loan up to $22,969

Prepayment Penalty (PPP) is considered as fee

- PPP period is 36 months or more
- PPP amount is 2% or more of the loan amount

Section 35 (High Priced Loan: HPML)

- Applies to purchase and refinance
- payment calculation: highest rate in first 5 years
- Section 35 loans must set-up impound account: Can't remove it for first 5 years
- Appraisal disclosure must be delivered within 3 days from loan application date

APR is higher than APOR

- 1st mortgage for conforming: 1.5%
- 1st mortgage loan amount over conforming limits: 2.5%
- Loans secured by a subordinate lien: 3.5%

Appraisal report is required except

- Streamline loans
- Manufactured homes
- Seller is government agency
- Purchasing foreclosed property

When two appraisal report is required

- Purchased within 90 days and new purchase price when up more than 10%
- Purchased over 90 days ago and new purchase price when up more than 20%

HMDA

- HMDA report is reported by the company who issues loan approval
- Min. of 4 reasons required for loan denial
- GFE record must be kept for 3 years from closing date
- When rate is locked, lender must send rate lock disclosure to the borrower(s)
- Lender must refund within 30 days from closing date for fee tolerance difference
- **Can't ask for any document unless LE is delivered to the borrower(s)**

TRID disclosure requirements

- name
- subject address
- income
- estimated value of the subject property
- loan amount
- social security number

Delivery days

- LE: within 3 business (open) days from application date
- CD: 3 business days before closing
  - not counting Sat, Sun, Legal holidays
  - for purchase: deliver to primary borrower
  - for refinance: deliver to all borrowers

Fee tolerance

- 10%
  - Recording fees
  - Charges paid to unaffiliated third-party service providers
- 0% tolerance
  - Origination fees (broker fee)
  - Lender fee
  - Transfer taxes

TILA (Record keeping period: 3 years)

Not allowed QM loans

- Neg. ARM

- Deferred loans
- balloon loans
- points and fees in excess of 3%

Timeline and delivery days

Purchase Transaction		Done by real estate agent	Done by MLO & processor
Days	**Action**	**Description**	
Prior to offer	Pre-approval	To determind loan amount & qualification	
	Offer made	Buyer sends purchase offer to seller	
Day 0	Contract signed	Contact is legally binding & fully enforceable	
Day 0-1	Escrow & Title	Listing agent opens escrow & title	
Day 1	Escrow & Title docs	Order Escrow Instruction & Title Report to Escrow	
Early as possible	Loan package prep.	Prepare Loan Package for submission to the lender	
Early as possible	Loan submission	Review loan package and submit for approval	
Day 1-7	Inspections	Home inspection is optional and paid by buyer. Termite inspection is usally paid by seller.	
Early as possible	Appraisal	Appraisal is ordered by The Lender paid by buyer	
Per contract	Contingency	Contingencys are removed per purchase contract (Usually Appraisal is 17 days & Loan is 20 days)	
After approval	Conditions	Request & prepare PTD conditions to order loan doc	
	Lock & Doc	Interest can be locked prior to PTD clearance. Loan doc can be ordered after clearance of PTD.	
	Doc sign	Loan doc need to be signed with public notary	
	Funding	Need to arrange funding date with selling agent	
	Funding	After clearance of PTF and review of loan docs, the lender will fund the loan	
Closing Date	Recording	Recording takes place 1 day after funding & same day recording is allowed by some county.	

Refinance Transaction | Done by MLO | Done by processor

Days	Action	Description
Day 0	Application	Loan application received
Within 3 days	Disclosures	Generate loan disclosures and get signed by borrowers
Day 0	Credit Report	Pull credit report for mortgage rating and debt verification. Credit reports are pulled by processors by some companies.
Day 0-1	Escrow & Title	Order Escrow Instruction & Title report through Escrow
Day 0-1	Borroewr docs	Request all necessary documents to borrower for verify with application
Early as possible	Loan package prep.	Prepare Loan Package for submission to the lender
Early as possible	Loan submission	Review loan package and submit for approval
	appraisal	Many loans don't require appraisal per DU findings. Need to wait for approval if it is required.
After approval	Conditions	Request & prepare PTD conditions to order loan doc
	Rate Lock	Interest can be locked prior to PTD clearance. Need to discuss rate lock with borrowers
	Loan Doc	Order loan doc to the lender after locking the rate
	Doc signing	Signing requires public notary to be present to verify borrowers for verification
	Funding	After clearance of PTF and review of loan docs, the lender will fund the loan
Closing Date	Recording	Recording takes place 3 day after funding. Borrowers have rights to cancel for 3 days for refinance transactions

Chapter 4.
LOAN DOCUMENTS

Licensing requirement

LO (loan originator) must have an NMLS license to perform.

LO's NMLS ID number must be listed on loan application and various documents.

Processors don't require any type of license.

Only time you require an NMLS license is when you run a processing company.

What makes a loan package

Following documents are needed for a submission package

- Loan application for borrower's personal information (1003)
- Loan summary sheet to explain loan information (1008)
- Credit report to check borrower's credit worthiness
- Income docs to check borrower's affordability
- Asset docs to check borrower's ability for down payment and / or closing cost

- Escrow instruction for transaction information
- Title report for subject property legality
- Additional docs to explain other issues like rental property, etc.
- Lender loan submission sheet

Documents for submission

Purchase Transaction

Documents	Who orders it	Where to get it
RPA (Purchase agreement)		Escrow Executed RPA with closing agent's information is required
Preliminary Report (Title report)	Listing agent opens title	Escrow
Escrow Instruction	Listing agent opens escrow	Escrow
EMD receipt (Initial deposit)		Escrow
EMD canceled check	Copy of canceled check or wire transaction history	LO & Borrower
Signed 1003 (Loan application)	LO (Loan originator)	LO & Borrower
1008 (Loan summary)	LO or Processor	
Signed Borrower authorization form	LO	LO & Borrower
Credit Card Authorization	LO	LO & Borrower
Credit report	LO or Processor	
Fee Sheet	LO or Processor	
Signed 4506-T	LO	LO & Borrower
Income documents	LO	LO & Borrower
Asset documents	LO	LO & Borrower

EOI (Evidence of Insurance)	Processor or Escrow	Escrow
* HOA Cert. (HOA Questionnaire)	Processor or Escrow	HOA
** Termite clearance cert.	Listing Agent	Escrow

*if applicable

**If termite inspection is waived by seller and buyer, escrow amendment must be provided

Refinance Transaction

Documents	Who orders it	Where to get it
Most recent mortgage statement	LO	Borrower
Preliminary Report (Title report)	LO or Escrow	Escrow
Escrow Instruction	LO	Escrow
Signed 1003 (Loan application)	LO (Loan originator)	LO & Borrower
1008 (Loan summary)	LO or Processor	
Signed Borrower authorization form	LO	LO & Borrowers
Credit Card Authorization	LO	LO & Borrowers
Credit report	LO or Processor	
Fee Sheet	LO or Processor	
Signed 4506-T	LO	LO & Borrowers
Income documents	LO	LO & Borrowers
Asset documents	LO	LO & Borrowers
EOI (Evidence of Insurance)	Processor or Escrow	Escrow
* HOA Cert. (HOA Questionnaire)	Processor or Escrow	HOA

*If applicable

How to hold title (California)

***Most mortgage lenders only allow natural persons and/or revocable trust only.**

Family Trust: Revocable trust can hold title but NOT Irrevocable trust.

Sole Ownership

Sole ownership may be described as ownership by an individual or other entity capable of acquiring title. Examples of common vesting cases of sole ownership are:

1. **A Single Man or Woman, an Unmarried Man or Woman or a Widow or Widower:**

A man or woman who is not legally married or in a domestic partnership. For example: Bruce Buyer, a single man.

2. **A Married Man or Woman as His or Her Sole and Separate Property:**

A married man or woman who wishes to acquire title in his or her name alone.

The title company insuring title will require the spouse of the married man or woman acquiring title to specifically disclaim or relinquish his or her right, title and interest to the property. This establishes that both spouses want title to the property to be granted to one spouse as that spouse's sole and separate property. The same rules will apply for same sex married couples. For example: Bruce Buyer, a married man, as his sole and separate property.

3. **A Domestic Partner as His or Her Sole and Separate Property:**

A domestic partner who wishes to acquire title in his or her name alone.

The title company insuring title will require the domestic partner of the person acquiring title to specifically disclaim or relinquish his or her right, title and interest to the property. This establishes that both domestic partners want title to the property to be granted to one partner as that person's sole and separate property. For example: Bruce Buyer, a registered domestic partner, as his sole and separate property.

Co-Ownership

Title to property owned by two or more persons may be vested in the following forms:

1. Community Property:

A form of vesting title to property owned together by married persons or by domestic partners. Community property is distinguished from separate property, which is property acquired before marriage or before a domestic partnership by separate gift or bequest, after legal separation, or which is agreed in writing to be owned by one spouse or domestic partner.

In California, real property conveyed to a married person, or to a domestic partner is presumed to be community property, unless otherwise stated (i.e. property acquired as separate property by gift, bequest or agreement). Since all such property is owned equally, both parties must sign all agreements and documents transferring the property or using it as security for a loan. Each owner has the right to dispose of his/her one half of the community property by will. For example: Bruce Buyer and Barbara Buyer, husband and wife, as community property, or Sally Smith and Jane Smith, registered domestic partners as community property. Another example for same sex couples: Sally Smith and Jane Smith, who are married to each other, as community property.

2. Community Property with Right of Survivorship:

A form of vesting title to property owned together by spouses or by domestic partners. This form of holding title shares many of the characteristics of community property but adds the benefit of the right of survivorship similar to title held in joint tenancy. There may be tax benefits for holding title in this manner. On the death of an owner, the decedent's interest ends and the survivor owns all interests in the property. For example: Bruce Buyer and Barbara Buyer, husband and wife, as community property with right of survivorship, or John Buyer and Bill Buyer, husband and husband, as community property with right of survivorship. Another example for same sex couples: Sally Smith and Jane Smith, registered domestic partners, as community property with right of survivorship.

3. Joint Tenancy:

A form of vesting title to property owned by two or more persons, who may or may not be married or domestic partners, in equal interests, subject to the right of survivorship in the surviving joint tenant(s). Title must have been acquired at the same time, by the same conveyance, and the document must expressly declare the intention to create a joint tenancy estate. When a joint tenant dies, title to the property is automatically conveyed by operation of law to the surviving joint tenant(s). Therefore, joint tenancy property is not subject to disposition by will. For example: Bruce Buyer, a married man and George Buyer, a single man, as joint tenants.

Note: If a married person enters into a joint tenancy that does not include their spouse, the title company insuring title may require the spouse of the married man or woman acquiring title to specifically consent to the joint tenancy. The same rules will apply for same sex married couples and domestic partners.

4. Tenancy in Common:

A form of vesting title to property owned by any two or more individuals in undivided fractional interests. These fractional interests may be unequal in quantity or duration and may arise at different times. Each tenant in common that owns a share of the property, is entitled to a comparable portion of the income from the property and must bear an equivalent share of expenses. Each co-tenant may sell, lease or will to his/her heir that share of the property belonging to him/her. For example: Bruce Buyer, a single man, as to an undivided 3/4 interest and Penny Purchaser, a single woman, as to an undivided 1/4 interest.

Items must be reviewed in documents

Income

- Pay-stubs
  - Name
  - Address
  - Social Security Number
  - Pay period for frequency of pay
  - Business name & address
- Personal Tax returns
  - Name
  - Current address
  - Social Security Number
  - Sch. 1 for other incomes
- Business Tax returns
  - Business type
  - Name
  - Business start year
  - Percentage of ownership

Asset

- Items must be verified from the Bank statements (all pages has to be included even if it is blank when there's page number)
    - Name
    - Mailing address
    - Large deposit (over $1,000 and more than 50% of the income)
    - Cash transactions
- Bank statement must have
    - The borrower as the account holder
    - Include at least 4 digits of the account number
    - Include the time period covered by the statement
    - Include all deposits and withdrawal transactions
    - Include all purchase and sale transactions
    - Include the ending account balance

Gift funds

- 100% gift is allowed for 1 unit principal residence for any LTV
- 100% gift is allowed for 1 to 4 unit principal residence & 2nd home for LTV ≤ 80%
- 5% borrower's own funds is required for 2 to 4 unit principal residence & 2nd home for LTV > 80%
- **Gift is not allowed for N.O.O.**

Reserves

Reserves are always determined by the DU findings.

- 6 months PITIA for NOO

- Acceptable Sources of Reserves
    - Checking or savings accounts
    - Investments in stocks, bonds, mutual funds, certificates of deposit, money market funds, and trust accounts
    - The amount vested in a retirement savings account
    - The cash value of vested life insurance policy
- Unacceptable Sources of Reserves
    - Funds that have not been vested
    - Funds that cannot be withdrawn under circumstances other than the account owner' s retirement,
    - employment termination, or death
    - Stock held in an unlisted corporation
    - Non-vested stock options and non-vested restricted stock
    - Personal unsecured loans
    - Interested party contributions (IPCs)
    - Any amount of lender contribution
    - Cash proceeds from a cash-out refinance transaction on the subject property
- Calculation of Reserves for Multiple Financed Properties
    - subject property, primary residence - per DU findings
    - Other financed properties
        - 2% of aggregate UPB if the borrower has one to four financed properties
        - 4% of aggregate UPB if the borrower has five to six financed properties
        - 6% of the aggregate UPB if the borrower has seven to ten financed properties

Must be indicated and verified items on documents

Loan Application

- Section 1: Borrower Information - Must verify with provided documents
- Section 2: Financial Information - Assets and Liabilities - Must get verifying documents
- Section 3: Financial Information - Real Estate - if applicable
- Section 4: Loan and Property Information - Subject property information
- Section 5: Declarations - All questions must be answered
- Section 6: Acknowledgments and Agreements - Borrower must sign and date (esign is allowed)
- Section 7: Military Service - if applicable
- Section 8: Demographic Information - required for HMDA report
- Section 9: Loan Originator Information - LO must sign and date

Credit Report

- Name, address, social security number
- Number of trade lines
- Length of trade lines
- Reported delinquencies
- Social security number check
- Reported address
- Reported employment
- Reported A.K.A.

Escrow Instruction

- Borrower Name
- Subject property address
- Contingency date
- Closing date
- Vesting

Preliminary Report (Title Report)

- Current owner's name
- Legal address (map address)
- Address
- Current liens against subject property
- Endorsements and easements

RPA (Residential Purchase Agreement)

- Contingency date for the loan
- Seller's name
- Buyer's name
- Purchase price
- Listing agent information
- Selling agent information
- Closing agent information

Appraisal Report

- Value of the subject property.
- Distance of the comps.
- Pictures for subject property to make sure property is in livable condition
- Pictures to meet compliance

What and how to review and verify

Loan Application (1003)

We will not discuss how to fill out 1003 since every loan origination software has different looks and ways.

However, all the fields on the applications are the same regardless of software.

Please practice with a printed form to be familiar with the 1003 form.

You need to review for sections and must verify:

- Personal information
- Employment and income
- Assets
- LO's NMLS status
- **All applicable fields must be filled out**
- Borrower and LO must sign and date

Section 1: Borrower Information. This section asks about your personal information and your income from employment and other sources, such as retirement, that you want considered to qualify for this loan.

1a. Personal Information

Name *(First, Middle, Last, Suffix)*

Alternate Names – *List any names by which you are known or any names under which credit was previously received (First, Middle, Last, Suffix)*

Social Security Number ___-___-___ *(or Individual Taxpayer Identification Number)*

Date of Birth *(mm/dd/yyyy)* ___/___/___

Citizenship
○ U.S. Citizen
○ Permanent Resident Alien
○ Non-Permanent Resident Alien

Type of Credit
○ I am applying for **individual credit.**
○ I am applying for **joint credit.** Total Number of Borrowers: ___
Each Borrower intends to apply for joint credit. **Your Initials:** ___

List Name(s) of Other Borrower(s) Applying for this Loan *(First, Middle, Last, Suffix) – Use a separator between names*

1b. Current Employment/Self-Employment and Income ☐ ***Does not apply***

Employer or Business Name ___ Phone (___) ___ - ___
Street ___ Unit # ___
City ___ State ___ ZIP ___ Country ___

Position or Title ___
Start Date ___/___/___ *(mm/dd/yyyy)*
How long in this line of work? ___ Years ___ Months

Check if this statement applies:
☐ I am employed by a family member, property seller, real estate agent, or other party to the transaction.

☐ **Check if you are the Business Owner or Self-Employed**
○ I have an ownership share of less than 25%.
○ I have an ownership share of 25% or more.
Monthly Income (or Loss) $ ___

Gross Monthly Income

Base	$	/month
Overtime	$	/month
Bonus	$	/month
Commission	$	/month
Military Entitlements	$	/month
Other	$	/month
TOTAL $	0	**/month**

Section 2: Financial Information — Assets and Liabilities.

This section asks about things you own that are worth money and that you want considered to qualify for this loan. It then asks about your liabilities (or debts) that you pay each month, such as credit cards, alimony, or other expenses.

2a. Assets – Bank Accounts, Retirement, and Other Accounts You Have

Include all accounts below. Under Account Type, choose from the types listed here:

- Checking
- Savings
- Money Market
- Certificate of Deposit
- Mutual Fund
- Stocks
- Stock Options
- Bonds
- Retirement *(e.g., 401k, IRA)*
- Bridge Loan Proceeds
- Individual Development Account
- Trust Account
- Cash Value of Life Insurance *(used for the transaction)*

Account Type – *use list above*	Financial Institution	Account Number	Cash or Market Value
			$
			$
			$
			$
			$
		Provide TOTAL Amount Here	$ 0

2c. Liabilities – Credit Cards, Other Debts, and Leases that You Owe

☐ ***Does not apply***

List all liabilities below (except real estate) and include deferred payments. Under Account Type, choose from the types listed here:

- Revolving *(e.g., credit cards)*
- Installment *(e.g., car, student, personal loans)*
- Open 30-Day *(balance paid monthly)*
- Lease *(not real estate)*
- Other

Account Type – *use list above*	Company Name	Account Number	Unpaid Balance	*To be paid off at or before closing*	Monthly Payment
			$	☐	$
			$	☐	$
			$	☐	$
			$	☐	$
			$	☐	$

Section 3: Financial Information — Real Estate.

This section asks you to list all properties you currently own and what you owe on them. ☐ ***I do not own any real estate***

3a. Property You Own

If you are refinancing, list the property you are refinancing FIRST.

Address Street ______ Unit # ______
City ______ State ______ ZIP ______ Country ______

Property Value	**Status:** Sold, Pending Sale, or Retained	**Intended Occupancy:** Investment, Primary Residence, Second Home, Other	**Monthly Insurance, Taxes, Association Dues, etc.** *if not included in Monthly Mortgage Payment*	**For 2-4 Unit Primary or Investment Property** Monthly Rental Income	**For LENDER to calculate:** Net Monthly Rental Income
$			$	$	$

Mortgage Loans on this Property ☐ ***Does not apply***

Creditor Name	Account Number	Monthly Mortgage Payment	Unpaid Balance	*To be paid off at or before closing*	**Type:** FHA, VA, Conventional, USDA-RD, Other	Credit Limit *(if applicable)*
		$	$	☐		$
		$	$	☐		$

Section 4: Loan and Property Information.

This section asks about the loan's purpose and the property you want to purchase or refinance.

4a. Loan and Property Information

Loan Amount $ ______ **Loan Purpose** ○ Purchase ○ Refinance ○ Other *(specify)* ______

Property Address Street ______ Unit # ______
City ______ State ______ ZIP ______ County ______
Number of Units ______ **Property Value** $ ______

Occupancy ○ Primary Residence ○ Second Home ○ Investment Property **FHA Secondary Residence** ☐

1. **Mixed-Use Property.** If you will occupy the property, will you set aside space within the property to operate your own business? *(e.g., daycare facility, medical office, beauty/barber shop)* ○ NO ○ YES
2. **Manufactured Home.** Is the property a manufactured home? *(e.g., a factory built dwelling built on a permanent chassis)* ○ NO ○ YES

Section 5: Declarations. This section asks you specific questions about the property, your funding, and your past financial history.

5a. About this Property and Your Money for this Loan

A. Will you occupy the property as your primary residence? If YES, have you had an ownership interest in another property in the last three years? If YES, complete (1) and (2) below: (1) What type of property did you own: primary residence (PR), FHA secondary residence (SR), second home (SH), or investment property (IP)? (2) How did you hold title to the property: by yourself (S), jointly with your spouse (SP), or jointly with another person (O)?	○ NO ○ YES ○ NO ○ YES
B. If this is a Purchase Transaction: Do you have a family relationship or business affiliation with the seller of the property?	○ NO ○ YES
C. Are you borrowing any money for this real estate transaction (*e.g., money for your closing costs or down payment*) or obtaining any money from another party, such as the seller or realtor, that you have not disclosed on this loan application? If YES, what is the amount of this money?	○ NO ○ YES $
D. 1. Have you or will you be applying for a mortgage loan on another property (not the property securing this loan) on or before closing this transaction that is not disclosed on this loan application? 2. Have you or will you be applying for any new credit (*e.g., installment loan, credit card, etc.*) on or before closing this loan that is not disclosed on this application?	○ NO ○ YES ○ NO ○ YES
E. Will this property be subject to a lien that could take priority over the first mortgage lien, such as a clean energy lien paid through your property taxes (*e.g., the Property Assessed Clean Energy Program*)?	○ NO ○ YES

Credit report

For mortgage loans, the credit report must be a tri merge credit report meaning all three credit bureaus information have to be on the report.

Three credit bureaus are Equifax, Experian and TransUnion.

Credit score and other factors determine the pricing (interest rate) of the loan transaction.

Some call credit scores FICO scores.

Credit report shows the borrower's payment behavior and that's what counts.

All lenders are expecting payments on time and that is the reason credit history is very important.

What to review in credit report

1. Borrower's information:

All information in the loan application has to match information in the credit report.

Applicant Information

Applicant: borrower name DOB: DOB SSN#: SSN
Street Address: current address Marital Status:
City, State, Zip: Own/Rent:
Length of Time: Dependants:
Property:

Applicant information section has the borrower's name, current address, date of birth and social security number.

If you pull a joint credit report for the husband and wife, both borrowers' information will be disclosed.

A joint credit report can only be pulled for husband and wife.

If there's multiple borrowers and if they are not husband and wife, the credit report has to be pulled separately.

2. **Credit Score:**

Higher the better always.

Most of the loan products require a minimum score of 620.

Higher scores always have better pricing.

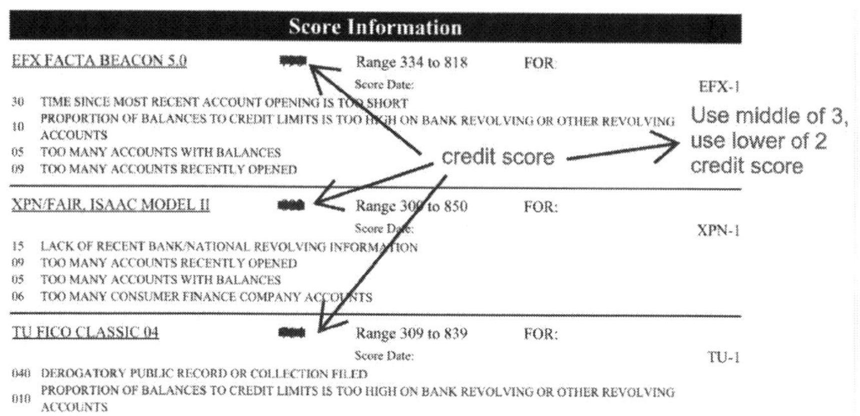

Score Information

EFX FACTA BEACON 5.0 Range 334 to 818 FOR:
Score Date: EFX-1
30 TIME SINCE MOST RECENT ACCOUNT OPENING IS TOO SHORT
10 PROPORTION OF BALANCES TO CREDIT LIMITS IS TOO HIGH ON BANK REVOLVING OR OTHER REVOLVING ACCOUNTS
05 TOO MANY ACCOUNTS WITH BALANCES
09 TOO MANY ACCOUNTS RECENTLY OPENED

XPN/FAIR, ISAAC MODEL II Range 300 to 850 FOR:
Score Date: XPN-1
15 LACK OF RECENT BANK/NATIONAL REVOLVING INFORMATION
09 TOO MANY ACCOUNTS RECENTLY OPENED
05 TOO MANY ACCOUNTS WITH BALANCES
06 TOO MANY CONSUMER FINANCE COMPANY ACCOUNTS

TU FICO CLASSIC 04 Range 309 to 839 FOR:
Score Date: TU-1
040 DEROGATORY PUBLIC RECORD OR COLLECTION FILED
010 PROPORTION OF BALANCES TO CREDIT LIMITS IS TOO HIGH ON BANK REVOLVING OR OTHER REVOLVING ACCOUNTS

Score information section shows the credit score for each credit bureaus.

- When there's three credit scores, the middle credit score is used for qualification.
- When there's two credit scores, the lower of two credit scores is used for qualification.
- When there's only one credit score, the borrower's credit is not good enough to qualify for the loan.

Example a:

Credit Scores	Credit Score for the Loan
700, 712, 723	712
722, 722, 724	722
722, 722, 711	722
734, 722	722

3. Employment information:

It is always better if employment on the loan application shows on the credit report.

Employment history section shows current employment.

Additional employment section shows current and / or previous employment information.

Employment Information	
Applicant	**Applicant**
Employer: current employment record	Employer:
Position Held:	Position Held:
Start/Stop Dates:	Start/Stop Dates:
Income:	Income:
Verified By/Date:	Verified By/Date:

Notice: This is a Merged report containing information supplied by the sources shown. The merge process is automated and the report may include some duplications and/or omissions.

Employment information section shows the current employment's name, address, and reported date.

4. Trade-lines

Each creditor's account is called a "trade line".

Reviewing trade-lines is very important. It is better if the borrower has more than three years of history with no lates and more than $5,000 credit limits.

Short credit history and low credit limit means the borrower has very weak credit.

Trade-lines show the borrower's behavior of making payments.

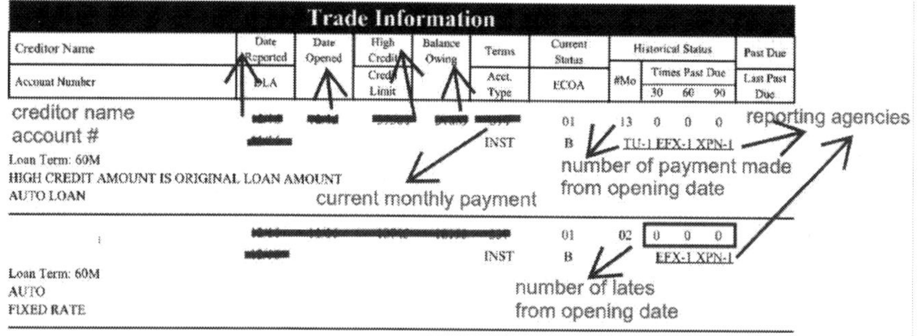

Trade information section has each creditor's name, account number, opening date, current payment status, current balance, highest credit amount, payment history, monthly payment amount, payment length and most importantly late payment history.

Most lender's prefer trade lines with over two year history with no lates.

Trade lines with less than $1,000 highest limit is a sign that the borrower has/had credit issues.

5. Collections, Public Record and Additional Employment Information

All collection accounts need to be paid off on or before closing except items listed under Fannie Mae guidelines, such as medical collections.

* Fannie Mae guidelines change frequently, make sure to check updates periodically.

Public records indicate the history of bankruptcy and more.

Bankruptcy history requirements vary per product.

Additional Employment Information lists may indicate current and / or previous employment information with dates.

Make sure to match information on loan application and employment history.

Make sure to check with the borrower if there's mis-match information.

Collection Information

Account Name	Date Reported	Date Opened	High Credit	Balance	Acct. Type	Account Status	Past Due
Account Number	Client				Credit Limit	ECOA	Last Past Due

collections will show here

Public Record Information

No Public Records exist in this section. BK will show here

Additional Employment Information

Current Employment - Applicant

Employer: emplyer name
emp. address

Type of Business:
Phone:
Position:

EFX-1

Salary or Wage:
Date Verified: reported date

Hire Date:
Verified By:

Date Discharged:
Title:

Former Employment - Applicant

Employer: previous employment history

Type of Business:
Phone:
Position:

EFX-1

Salary or Wage:
Date Verified:

Hire Date:
Verified By:

Date Discharged:
Title:

6. Additional Address Information

Additional address information section shows current and / or previous addresses for the borrower.

If the current address on loan application and additional address information section doesn't match, you MUST check with the borrower for occupancy issues that can be raised by the underwriter.

Additional Address Information								
Current Address(es)								
Date Reported	Move In Date	Move Out Date	Length of Time	Rent Amount	Unit Number	Own/Rent/ Other	Number of Lates	Balance

current address TU-1

Landlord/Mortgage Company: Phone:
Verified Date: Verified By:

EFX-1 XPN-1

Landlord/Mortgage Company: Phone:
Verified Date: Verified By:

Former Address(es)								
Date Reported	Move In Date	Move Out Date	Length of Time	Rent Amount	Unit Number	Own/Rent/ Other	Number of Lates	Balance

previous address EFX-1 TU-1

Landlord/Mortgage Company: Phone:
Verified Date: Verified By:

7. Inquiries

You must check with the borrower for the inquiries made within 120 days of the loan application date.

- Must check if there's any open account for the inquiries for the payment shock
- Must get LOEs (Letter of explanation) for each inquiry made

Inquiries In the last 90 days
company name & date TU-1

8. A.K.A. (Also Known As)

AKA shows the other names the borrower used.

Many people use first names and last names but some companies require you to put a middle initial or full middle name.

For example, John Doe, John S. Doe, John Smith Doe. etc.

The following AKA(s) were reported		
Name	SSN #	DOB

"Also Known As" names XPN-1

Liabilities

Credit Cards

- Use the payment on credit report.
- Credit card without payment amount.
    - o Copy of a most recent statement showing monthly payment can be used.
    - o Use 5% of the outstanding balance.

Student Loans

- If a monthly payment shows on the credit report, use it.
- For differed student loan, use 1% of the outstanding balance as payment.

Federal Income Tax Installment Agreements

Borrower's monthly payment on an installment agreement with the IRS need to be counted as the borrower's monthly debt obligations.

Required documents:

- an approved IRS installment agreement with the terms of re-payment, including the monthly payment amount and total amount due.
- evidence of payments.

Acceptable evidence includes the most recent payment reminder from the IRS, reflecting the last payment amount and date and the next payment amount owed and due date. At least one payment must have been made prior to closing.

Garnishments

All garnishments with more than 10 months remaining must be included in the borrower's recurring monthly debt obligations.

Home Equity Lines of Credit

- Use the payment on the credit report.
- If current balance is $0, don't need to hit any payment.
- If the payment doesn't show, hit 5% of balance showing on credit report.

Lease Payments

Lease payments must be considered as recurring monthly debt obligations regardless of the number of months remaining on the lease.

Installment for automobile loan

Loan payments be omitted if less than 10 payments remain.

Open 30-Day Charge Accounts

- Open 30-day charge accounts require the balance to be paid in full every month.
- Open 30-day charge accounts are not required to be included in the DTI ratio.

Escrow instruction

Purchase transaction escrow instruction indicates "closing date", "Purchase price" and "EMD amount" which will not be on refinance transaction.

Closing date is the date the loan MUST be closed per purchase agreement between seller and buyer.

Missing the closing date can cause cancellation of transaction or additional penalty fees.

Escrow instruction for purchase transaction

ESCROW IS AN INDEPENDENT ESCROW COMPANY OPERATING UNDER A LICENSE FROM THE CALIFORNIA DEPARTMENT OF FINANCIAL PROTECTION AND INNOVATION, LICENSE NUMBER

ESCROW OFFICER: DATE:
ESCROW NO:

SUPPLEMENTAL SALE ESCROW INSTRUCTIONS

I/We, the undersigned Buyers and Seller (collectively "Parties"), hand date Escrow, (Escrow Holder"), a copy of the California Residential Purchase Agreement and Joint Escrow Instructions Dated date and Seller Counter Offer No. 1 dated date ("Purchase Agreement"), which are incorporated by reference and shall serve as escrow instructions when executed and legible. Unless Escrow Holder gives written notice, it will not perform certain acts in the Purchase Agreement. Escrow Holder's duties are limited to those paragraphs in the Purchase Agreement identifying its responsibilities and the duties set forth in these Supplemental Sale Escrow Instructions and the General Provisions ("Escrow Instructions"). All other terms and conditions in the Purchase Agreement are between Buyer(s), Seller(s), and their respective brokers only. Escrow Holder is not to be concerned with, or liable for, any obligations, express, implied, or equitable among the Buyer(s), Seller(s), or their real estate broker(s) in the Purchase Agreement.

If a conflict arises between the terms of the Purchase Agreement and any Escrow Instructions, the Purchase Agreement shall govern as between the Buyer(s) and Seller(s). The Escrow Instructions shall govern the duties and obligations of Escrow Holder.

THE ADDITIONAL ESCROW INSTRUCTIONS AND TERMS ("GENERAL PROVISIONS") ARE ATTACHED AND INCORPORATED BY THIS REFERENCE. THE UNDERSIGNED ACKNOWLEDGE THEY HAVE RECEIVED, READ, AND UNDERSTAND THE GENERAL PROVISIONS AND APPROVE, ACCEPT, AND AGREE TO BE BOUND BY THEM.

The following is restated from the Purchase Agreement:

Buyer has deposited with Escrow Holder an initial deposit of
Buyer will execute and deliver a New Deed of Trust in the amount of
Prior to close of escrow, Buyer will deposit in the manner called for herein, an additional amount of
PURCHASE PRICE (TOTAL)

CLOSE OF ESCROW ON or before: ← closing date → 12/12/20

The undersigned will deliver to Escrow Holder any instruments or funds required for it to comply with these Escrow Instructions, all of which it may use, provided that, by Close of Escrow, it has received a preliminary report from a title company committing to issue a policy of title insurance as required under the Purchase Agreement with the title company's exceptions on the real property in the County of Los Angeles, State of California described as:

LEGAL DESCRIPTION RECEIVED IS ATTACHED AS EXHIBIT "A" AND IS MADE A PART HEREOF

SELLER STATES THE PROPERTY ADDRESS IS: subject property address

TITLE SHALL BE VESTED IN: vesting **...complete vesting to follow**

(Buyer shall provide Escrow Holder a complete vesting during escrow. Escrow Holder is authorized and instructed to correct the grant deed being delivered in the above numbered escrow to reflect the vesting designated by Buyer, over the notarized signature of Seller thereon, with no further authorization required.)

Escrow instruction for refinance transaction

ESCROW CO.

REFINANCE ESCROW INSTRUCTIONS

escrow officer name
Sr. Escrow Officer

ESCROW NO.: esc.no.
DATE: date

Lender will hand you the proceeds of **new first trust deed in the amount of $** loan amount less lender's normal costs and charges, which you are authorized to use on or before lender's request provided upon recordation of the securing Deed of Trust, you obtain an A.L.T.A. Loan policy of title insurance per lender's requirements covering real property in the County of Orange, CA, described as follows:

LEGAL DESCRIPTION ATTACHED HERETO AS EXHIBIT "A" AND MADE A PART HEREOF

APN: APN (parcel number)

Property Address (not verified): subject property address

Showing Title Vested in: vesting per borrower

You are instructed and authorized to obtain policy of title insurance from any reliable title company.

SUBJECT TO:

(1) All General and Special Taxes for the fiscal year 2020-2021, including any special levies, payments for which are included therein and collected therewith for the current fiscal year, not delinquent, and taxes for the ensuring year, if any, a lien but not yet payable.

(2) Bonds-assessments: none

(3) All taxes, bonds, and assessments levied or assessed subsequent to date of these instructions.

(4) Covenants, conditions, restrictions, reservations, rights, rights of way, and easements, and kindred substances on or under said land, now of record, if any.

(5) First Deed of Trust to record securing a note in the amount of $ loan amount

INSTRUCTIONS:

1. BORROWER to furnish, when required, a new fire insurance policy satisfactory to the new lender and authorizes payment of bill, if presented in escrow.

2. Borrower's execution of all lender's documents shall deem borrower's full approval of all terms and conditions contained therein and escrow holder shall not be further concerned therewith.

3. Deposit of Lender's funds will evidence their approval of the terms and conditions contained herein.

(CONTINUED)

Borrower's Initials: ____/____ Borrower's Initials: ____/____

Title report

Title report, Schedule A, has legal owners' name.

Your Reference No:

Property Address: subject property address

PRELIMINARY REPORT

SCHEDULE A

The form of policy of title insurance contemplated by this report is:

ALTA Loan 2006

The estate or interest in the land hereinafter described or referred to covered by this report is:

A Fee ← Has to be "Fee". "Lease holds" has restrictions

Title to said estate or interest at the date hereof is vested in:

John Doe and Jane Doe, husband and wife as community property with right of survivorship Current owner's name

The land referred to herein is situated in the County of Riverside, State of California, and is described as follows:

SEE EXHIBIT "A" ATTACHED HERETO AND MADE A PART HEREOF

Schedule B shows a list of liens against the property.

SCHEDULE B – Section B

4. A deed of trust to secure an indebtedness in the amount shown below, and any other obligations secured thereby

Amount:	$300,000.00
Dated:	September 23, 2010
Trustor/Grantor:	John Doe and Jane Doe, husband and wife
Trustee:	ABC
Beneficiary:	Mortgage Electronic Registration Systems, Inc., solely as nominee for AAA Mortgage, its successors and assigns Loan
No.:	Not Set Out
Recorded Date:	September 30, 2010
Recorded No:	2010-1234567, of Official Records

Income documents

How to calculate income is very important. It will determine if the borrower qualifies for the loan.

You need to know exactly what types of documents are needed for types of employment.

Income documents differ by the type of employment. Please refer to the table below.

Wage Earner

W-2	Most recent two years
Pay stubs	Most recent one full month

Self-Employer

*If borrower has 25% or more ownership, borrower is considered as "self-employed".

**Due to Covid-19, current guideline requires additional documents.

Ownership Type	Documents
Sole proprietorship	Most recent two years Personal Tax Returns
Partnership, Limited liability partnership, S Corporation	Most recent two years; • Personal Tax Returns • Business Tax Returns • K-1s • W-2s, if applicable
C corporation	Most recent two years; • Personal Tax Returns • Business Tax Returns • W-2s, if applicable
**All self-employed borrower (These are supporting documents not used as an income documents)	• Year to Date P & L statement • Most recent three months bank statements

How to calculate income

Most recent 2 years of employment history is required for all borrowers to use income.

If current employment history is less than 2 years, previous employment must be the same line of business and same job descriptions or the borrower must have graduated less than 2 years and need to provide a graduation certificate as a proof.

If a wage earner is getting paid other than base salary such as tips or bonuses, additional income must be received for the most recent 2 years and must be averaged out to a month from most recent 2 years W-2 forms as income amount. Can't use the current amount.

If the borrower is getting housing allowances and /or military subsidies, the borrower must provide a letter to ensure that income will be continued for at least next 3 years from the employer.

For wage earners, you just need the most recent pay-stubs to cover one whole month.

For self-employed borrowers, average income is used for most recent two years tax returns if income is increasing. Most recent years tax return's income is used if the income is declining.

Pay stubs

Gross income is used in the mortgage loan for qualification.

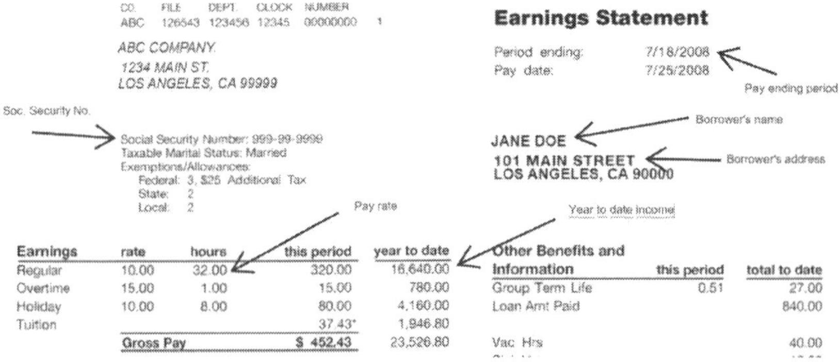

CO.	FILE	DEPT.	CLOCK	NUMBER	
ABC	126543	123456	12345	0000000	1

ABC COMPANY.
1234 MAIN ST.
LOS ANGELES, CA 99999

Earnings Statement

Period ending: 7/18/2008
Pay date: 7/25/2008

Social Security Number: 999-99-9999
Taxable Marital Status: Married
Exemptions/Allowances:
Federal: 3, $25 Additional Tax
State: 2
Local: 2

JANE DOE
101 MAIN STREET
LOS ANGELES, CA 90000

Earnings	rate	hours	this period	year to date
Regular	10.00	32.00	320.00	16,640.00
Overtime	15.00	1.00	15.00	780.00
Holiday	10.00	8.00	80.00	4,160.00
Tuition			37.43*	1,946.80
	Gross Pay		$ 452.43	23,526.80

Other Benefits and Information	this period	total to date
Group Term Life	0.51	27.00
Loan Amt Paid		840.00
Vac Hrs		40.00

Pay period

Must get pay stubs to cover **the most recent one full month** pay stubs.

If the pay period only shows the ending date, you must get prior pay stub to check pay duration.

Ways to calculate monthly income

Monthly (once a month) = Gross Pay Amount of the pay stub

- Semi-monthly (twice a month) = Gross Pay Amount x 2
- Bi-weekly (pay every other week) = Gross Pay Amount x 26 ÷ 12
- Weekly (pay every week) = Gross Pay Amount x 52 ÷ 12

Must check items

- Borrower's name
- Borrower's home address
- Social Security Number
- Must compare pay stub's total pay amount with year to date to confirm pay amount
- Company Name & Address

Tax Returns

To calculate income for self-employed borrowers, Fannie Mae uses Fannie Mae form 1084 (Cash Flow Analysis),

Form 1084 has to be used for all self-employed borrowers and each company borrower owns.

If the borrower owns two companies called ABC and XYZ, form 1084 has to be used twice.

One for ABC and one for XYZ.

Use W-2 income from ABC on form 1084 for ABC only, can't be used in form 1084 for XYZ.

For rental income, use form 1037 and/or 1038.

Liquidity tests must be done if the nature of the business requires inventory.

Per Fannie Mae guideline, only distribution on form K-1 can be used as income but if business passes liquidity test, ordinary income can be used even if there's no distributions.

Tax Returns by type

*All tax returns must include all the schedules if applicable.

Type	Tax Returns with all Schedules
Personal	1040, Rental income: Sch. E
Sole proprietorship	1040 with Sch. C
Partnership	1065 with Sch. K-1
Limited Liability Partnership	1120 or 1065 with Sch. K-1
S Corporation	1120S with Sch. K-1
C Corporation	1120

Tax returns are used to calculate income for the self-employed borrowers.

Due to the different types of business structure, tax returns differ as well.

For all self-employed borrowers, personal & business income taxes are required to calculate income for the borrower.

Make sure to get copies of W-2s if applicable.

How to fill out Form 1084

Fannie Mae **Cash Flow Analysis (Form 1084)**

This form must be used to calculate self-emp.'s income for each company owns.

Only use stable income. DO NOT use one time income. **Borrower Name:** ____________________

Make sure to put company name. *Business Name (optional):* ________________________________

This worksheet may be used to prepare a written evaluation of the analysis of income related to self-employment. The purpose of this written analysis is to determine the amount of stable and continuous income that will be available to the borrower for loan qualifying purposes.

If the income is decreasing, use year for the less income.
If the income is increasing, use two years average income.

IRS Form 1040 – Individual Income Tax Return **Year**________ **Year**________

1. **W-2 Income from Self-Employment** Box 5 on W-2 from company listed on top only.

2. **Schedule B – Interest and Ordinary Dividends** Don't use Sch. B income if possible. It is NOT easy to prove stable income.
   a. Interest Income from Self-Employment Line 1
   b. Dividends from Self-Employment Line 5

3. **Schedule C – Profit or Loss from Business: Sole Proprietorship**
   a. Net Profit or (Loss) line 31
   b. Nonrecurring Other (Income) Loss/Expenses line 6 (other income). - Nonrecurring income must be deducted from the income since it is an one time income.
   c. Depletion line 12
   d. Depreciation line 13
   e. Non-deductible Travel and Meals Expenses line 24b
   f. Business Use of Home line 30
   g. Amortization/Casualty Loss Part V (pg 2), use AMORTIZATION only

4. **Schedule D – Capital Gains and Losses** Don't use if possible.
   a. Recurring Capital Gains Part II, line 15 - has to be recurring

5. **Schedule E – Supplemental Income and Loss**

Note: A lender may use Fannie Mae Rental Income Worksheets (Form 1037 or Form 1038) to calculate individual rental income (loss) reported on Schedule E.

   ~~a. Royalties Received~~
   ~~b. Total Expenses~~
   ~~c. Depletion~~

For "Schedule E" income, use rental income analysis forms, don't use a, b, c below.

6. **Schedule F – Profit or Loss from Farming** Most of California loans don't apply.
   a. Net Farm Profit or (Loss)
   b. Non-Tax Portion Ongoing Coop and CCC Payments
   c. Nonrecurring Other (Income) Loss
   d. Depreciation
   e. Amortization/Casualty Loss/Depletion
   f. Business Use of Home

Note: IRS Form 4797 (Sales of Business Property) is not included on this worksheet due to its infrequent use. If applicable, a lender may include analysis of the sale and related recurring capital gains.

Partnership or S Corporation

A self-employed borrower's share of Partnership or S Corporation earnings can only be considered if the lender obtains documentation, such as Schedule K-1, verifying that

- the income was actually distributed to the borrower, or
- the business has adequate liquidity to support the withdrawal of earnings. If the Schedule K-1 provides this confirmation, no further documentation of business liquidity is required.

Note: See the Instructions for additional guidance on documenting access to income and business liquidity.

IRS Form 1065 - Partnership Income

7. **Schedule K-1 Form 1065 – Partner's Share of Income** **Year__________** **Year__________**
   a. Ordinary Income (Loss) line 1(ordinary income) or 19(distribution) - if there's no distribution and liquidity test doesn't pass, ordinary income can NOT be used.
   b. Net Rental Real Estate; Other Net Income (Loss) line 2 & 3
   c. Guaranteed Payments to Partner line 4c

Ordinary income can be used if liquidity test passes and there's no distribution

*Liquidity test must be done if the nature of business requires inventory.

8. **Form 1065 - Adjustments to Business Cash Flow**
   a. Ordinary (Income) Loss from Other Partnerships line 4
   b. Nonrecurring Other (Income) Loss line 5, 6, 7
   c. Depreciation line 16c + line 14 from form 8825
   d. Depletion line 17
   e. Amortization/Casualty Loss line 20, use AMORTIZATION only
   f. Mortgages or Notes Payable in Less than 1 Year Sch. L, line 16d
   g. Non-deductible Travel and Entertainment Expenses Sch. M-1, line 4b
   h. Subtotal
   i. Total Form 1065
   (Subtotal multiplied by % of ownership) If the borrower has 50% ownership, use 50% of income________

IRS Form 1120S – S Corporation Earnings **Year__________** **Year__________**

9. **Schedule K-1 Form 1120S – Shareholder's Share of Income**
   a. Ordinary Income (Loss) line 1(ordinary income) or 19(distribution) - if there's no distribution and liquidity test doesn't pass, ordinary income can NOT be used.
   b. Net Rental Real Estate; Other Net Rental Income (Loss) line 2 & 3

Ordinary income can be used if liquidity test passes and there's no distribution

*Liquidity test must be done if the nature of business requires inventory.

10. **Form 1120S - Adjustments to Business Cash Flow**
   a. Nonrecurring Other (Income) Loss line 4 & 5
   b. Depreciation line 14 & line 14 from form 8825
   c. Depletion line 15
   d. Amortization/Casualty Loss line 19
   e. Mortgages or Notes Payable in Less than 1 Year Sch. L, line 17d
   f. Non-deductible Travel and Entertainment Expenses Sch. M-1, line 3d
   g. Subtotal
   h. Total Form 1120S
   (Subtotal multiplied by % of ownership) If the borrower has 50% ownership, use 50% of income________

IRS Form 1120 – Regular Corporation

Corporation earnings may be used when the borrower(s) own 100% of the corporation.

Year__________ **Year__________**

11. **Form 1120 – Regular Corporation**
   a. Taxable Income line 30
   b. Total Tax line 31
   c. Nonrecurring (Gains) Losses line 8 & 9
   d. Nonrecurring Other (Income) Loss line 10
   e. Depreciation line 20
   f. Depletion line 21
   g. Amortization/Casualty Loss line 26 (other deduction)
   h. Net Operating Loss and Special Deductions line 29c
   i. Mortgages or Notes Payable in Less than 1 Year Sch. L, line 17d
   j. Non-deductible Travel and Entertainment Expenses Sch. M-1, line 5c
   k. Subtotal
   l. Less: Dividends Paid to Borrower form 1040, Sch. B
   m. Total Form 1120

For "Depletion" and "other deductions", make sure to check statements and only add back "AMORTIZATION"

Chapter 5.

MATRIX AND RATE SHEET

How to read matrix

Sample matrix

Min Fico	Unit	Max Loan Amt	Max LTV/CLTV	
			Purchase & R/T	Cash-Out
620	1 Unit	647,200	*DU: 97% LP: 95%	80%
	2 Unit	828,700	85%	75%
	3 Unit	1,001,650	75%	75%
	4 Unit	1,244,850	75%	75%

LTV: Loan to Value

CLTV: Combined Loan to Value

HCLTV: High Credit Loan to Value (original loan amount, full amount of any HELOCs, and the unpaid principal balance of all closed-end Loans to Value)

FRM: Fixed Rate Mortgage

ARM: Adjustable Rate Mortgage

Each program has its own matrix.

Example a

Sam is purchasing a home as owner occupied, a condo for $500,000 with $100,000 down.

Purchase price = $500,000

Down payment = $100,000

Loan amount = $400,000

LTV = 400,000 (loan amount) ÷ 500,000 (purchase price) = 80%

Property = Condo = 1 unit

Principal Residence		
Purchase Limited Cash-Out Refinance	1 Unit	FRM: 97% (1) ARM: 95%
	2 Units	FRM/ARM: 85%
	3-4 Units	FRM/ARM: 75%

Owner occupied = Principal Residence - okay

Property = 1 unit (all condos are 1 unit) - okay

LTV = 80% - okay (max. LTV is 97%)

*Borrower DOES qualify for conforming 30 year fixed program.

Example b

Sarah is purchasing a 3 units property as owner occupied for $500,000 with $100,000 down.

Purchase price = $500,000

Down payment = $100,000

Loan amount = $400,000

LTV = 400,000 (loan amount) ÷ 500,000 (purchase price) = 80%

Property = 3 unit

Principal Residence		
Purchase Limited Cash-Out Refinance	1 Unit	FRM: 97% (1) ARM: 95%
	2 Units	FRM/ARM: 85%
	3-4 Units	FRM/ARM: 75%

Owner occupied = Principal Residence - okay

Property = 3 units - okay

LTV = 80% - Not okay (max. LTV is 75% for 3 units)

*Borrower DOES NOT qualify for conforming 30 year fixed program.

How to read rate sheet

Rate & Pricing

When the borrower is not paying nor getting lender's credit, it is called par pricing.

There are two ways to post rate price. Starting base price from:

- 0 (zero) or;
- 100

Par pricing is published as 0.000 or 100.000 depending on lenders.

Here's how lenders are publishing price for each rate

- Par = 0.000 = 100.000
- Lender's credit of 0.5% (of the loan amount) = (0.500) = 100.500
- Borrower pays of 0.5% (of the loan amount) = 0.500 = 99.500

You must know how to read the rate sheet and price the loan.

- All pricing and add-ons are a percentage of the loan amount.
- Lock days means that the rate you lock is good for the period (calendar days) from the date you locked.
- Longer the lock period, worse the price

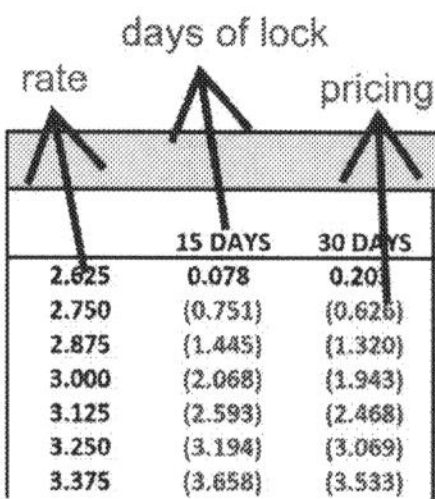

	15 DAYS	30 DAYS
2.625	0.078	0.20[illegible]
2.750	(0.751)	(0.62[illegible])
2.875	(1.445)	(1.320)
3.000	(2.068)	(1.943)
3.125	(2.593)	(2.468)
3.250	(3.194)	(3.069)
3.375	(3.658)	(3.533)

*( ) : credit to borrower

*No parenthesis: cost to borrower

Add-ons for the program

Add-ons are fees for credit score, LTV, property types, etc. per program.

Add-ons are differed by the program.

If the borrower has good credit score with low LTV, the borrower will get lower rates than a borrower with higher LTV and lower credit score.

Example a

Sam is purchasing a home as owner occupied, a house for $500,000 with $100,000 down and his credit score is 702.

Purchase price = $500,000

Down payment = $100,000

Loan amount = $400,000

LTV = 400,000 (loan amount) ÷ 500,000 (purchase price) = 80%

Property = 1 unit house

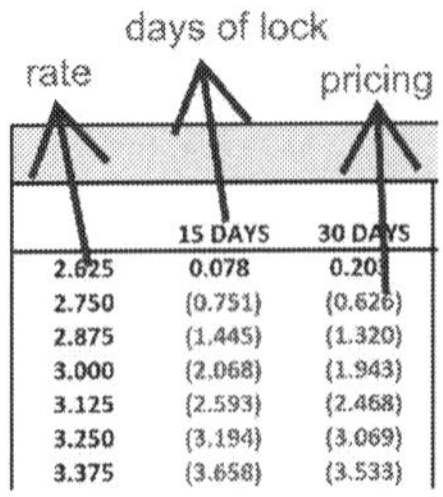

	15 DAYS	30 DAYS
2.625	0.078	0.20[illegible]
2.750	(0.751)	(0.626)
2.875	(1.445)	(1.320)
3.000	(2.068)	(1.943)
3.125	(2.593)	(2.468)
3.250	(3.194)	(3.069)
3.375	(3.658)	(3.533)

par pricing = 0 cost & 0 credit

Table 1: All Eligible Mortgages – LLPA by Credit Score/LTV Ratio

Representative Credit Score	LTV Range Applicable for all mortgages with terms greater than 15 years									
	≤ 60.00%	60.01 – 70.00%	70.01 – 75.00%	75.01 – 80.00%	80.01 – 85.00%	85.01 – 90.00%	90.01 – 95.00%	95.01 – 97.00%	>97.00%	SFC
≥ 740	0.000%	0.250%	0.250%	0.500%	0.250%	0.250%	0.250%	0.750%	0.750%	N/A
720 – 739	0.000%	0.250%	0.500%	0.750%	0.500%	0.500%	0.500%	1.000%	1.000%	N/A
700 – 719	0.000%	0.500%	1.000%	1.250%	1.000%	1.000%	1.000%	1.500%	1.500%	N/A
680 – 699	0.000%	0.500%	1.250%	1.750%	1.500%	1.250%	1.250%	1.500%	1.500%	N/A
660 – 679	0.000%	1.000%	2.250%	2.750%	2.750%	2.250%	2.250%	2.250%	2.250%	N/A
640 – 659	0.500%	1.250%	2.750%	3.000%	3.250%	2.750%	2.750%	2.750%	2.750%	N/A
620 – 639	0.500%	1.500%	3.000%	3.000%	3.250%	3.250%	3.250%	3.500%	3.500%	N/A
< 620[1]	0.500%	1.500%	3.000%	3.000%	3.250%	3.250%	3.250%	3.750%	3.750%	N/A

Borrower has 702 credit score and 80% LTV. Select the section for that and it has 1.25% add-ons.

Pricing example a

2.875% rate has (1.32) for 30 days lock

(1.320) credit + 1.25 cost (add-ons) = (0.070) credit to the borrower

$400,000 x 0.070% = $280 credit to the borrower

Pricing example b

2.750% rate has (0.626) for 30 days lock

(0.626) credit + 1.25 cost (add-ons) = 0.624 cost to the borrower

$400,000 x 0.624% = $2,496 cost to the borrower

= borrower needs to come in with additional pricing fee of $2,496

Chapter 6.
BASIC FANNIE MAE GUIDELINES

(as of 8/20/2022)

How to know if borrower qualifies

Many people don't realize there are many mortgage programs for borrowers with different financial situations.

Even Fannie Mae Conforming programs have many different programs to suit each borrower's financial situations.

To qualify for the loan, the borrower must meet program guidelines.

LOs and processors must know basic guidelines for each program.

To be successful in the mortgage industry, you must know the Fannie Mae Selling Guide.

Before you check program matrix

you must have basic loan scenario to find the right program

- Borrower's legal status
- Income document type

- Loan purpose
- Loan term
- Loan amount
- Is there 'subordinate loan'
- Property type
- Occupancy type
- LTV
- Credit score
- Asset and reserves
- Is there 'Gift"
- DTI

See below simple diagram to find program

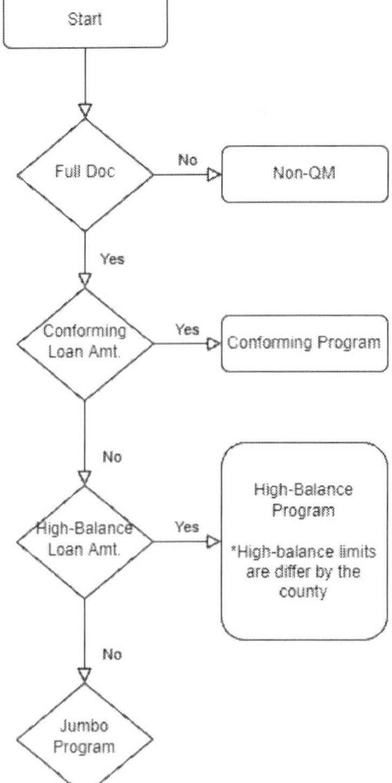

After selecting the program by the loan amount, you must check the program matrix for other items for qualification such as occupancy type, property type, LTV, etc.

Even for full doc loans, you have the option to use Non-QM programs for other reasons.

DTI (Debt to Income ratio)

Why is the DTI ratio so important and how to calculate DTI?

Rule of thumb for max DTI ratio is 43% for conventional loans. Over 43% is allowed up to 50% per DU findings with restrictions.

DTI ratio = Total Expenses ÷ Total Gross Income

Total expenses = proposed monthly housing expenses + total monthly minimum payments showing on credit report

Housing expenses (monthly) = monthly mortgage payment + monthly home insurance + monthly property taxes + monthly HOA dues (if applicable)

Total monthly minimum payments on credit report include credit cards, auto loans, student loans, installment loans, etc.

Example a
Monthly gross income = $10,000
Income = $10,000
Monthly mortgage payment = $2,000
Monthly property tax = $800
Monthly home insurance = $100
Housing expenses = $2,900
Total monthly minimum credit card payments = $500
Total monthly minimum installment payments = $1,200
Other expenses = $1,700
(housing expenses + other expenses) ÷ income = DTI
(2,900 + 1,700) ÷ 10,000 = 46% DTI

Limits on the Number of financed Properties

Subject Property Occupancy	Transaction	Maximum Number of Financed Properties
Principal residence	Transactions other than HomeReady loans	No limit
Principal residence	HomeReady loans	DU and manually underwritten - 2
Second home or Investment property	All	DU - 10

Income

IRS Forms

IRS Form Number	Title
Form 990	Return of Organization Exempt From Income Tax Form
Form 1040	U.S. Individual Income Tax Return
Form 1040, Schedule B	Interest and Ordinary Dividends
Form 1040, Schedule C	Profit or Loss from Business (Sole Proprietorship)
Form 1040, Schedule D	Capital Gains and Losses
Form 1040, Schedule E	Supplemental Income and Loss
Form 1040, Schedule F	Profit or Loss From Farming
Form 1065	U.S. Return of Partnership Income
Form 1065, Schedule K-1	Partner's Share of Income, Deductions, Credits, etc.
Form 1099-A	Acquisition or Abandonment of Secured Property
Form 1099-C	Cancellation of Debt
Form 1099-DIV	Dividends and Distributions
Form 1099-MISC	Miscellaneous Income
Form 1120	U.S. Corporation Income Tax Return
Form 1120-S	U.S. Income Tax Return for an S Corporation
Form 1120-S, Schedule K-1	Shareholder's Share of Income, Deductions, Credits, etc.
Form 2106	Employee Business Expenses

Form 4506-C	IVES Request for Transcript of Tax Return
Form 4797	Sales of Business Property
Form 6252	Installment Sale Income
Form 8825	Rental Real Estate Income and Expenses of a Partnership or an S Corporation
Form W-4	Employee's Withholding Allowance Certificate

Income Types

- Wage Earner
- Self-Employed (anyone with 25% or more ownership considered as Self-emp.)

Business Structure for Self-Employed Borrower(s)

Sole Proprietorships

- An unincorporated business that is individually owned and managed.
- Income docs: Form 1040, Schedule C

Partnerships

- General Partnership
  - o Each partner has responsibility for running the business
- Limited Partnership
  - o A limited partner has limited liability based on the amount he or she invested in the partnership
- Income docs: Form 1065, Schedule K-1

Limited Liability Companies (LLC)

- A hybrid business structure that is designed to offer its member-owners the tax efficiencies of partnership and the limited liability advantages of a corporation
- Income docs: Schedule K-1, Form 1065 or Form 1120s

S Corporations

- A legal entity that has a limited number of stockholders and elects not to be taxed as a regular corporation
- Income docs: Form 1120S, Schedule K-1

Corporations

- A state-chartered legal entity that exists separately and distinctly from its owners. It is the most flexible form of business organization for purposes of obtaining capital.
- income docs: Form 1120

Verification of Base Pay, Bonus, and Overtime Income

- A minimum history of 2 years of employment income is recommended.
- Borrowers relying on overtime or bonus income for qualifying purposes must have a history of no less than 24 months to be considered stable.

Income document requirements

Base Pay

- Most recent 1 month pay stub and most recent 2 years' W-2s
- Verification of Employment (VOE form, Form 1005) – optional

Bonus or Overtime

- Most recent 1 month pay stub and most recent 2 years' W-2s
- Verification of Employment (VOE form, Form 1005) with breakdown of incomes

Commission Income

- Minimum of 2 years of commission income is required
- Most recent 1 month pay stub and most recent 2 years' W-2s

- Verification of Employment (VOE form, Form 1005) with breakdown of incomes

Tip Income

- Minimum of 2 years of tip income is required
- Most recent 1 month pay stub and most recent 2 years' W-2s
- Verification of Employment (VOE form, Form 1005) with breakdown of incomes
- Must verify that the borrower has received it for at least for the last two years

Secondary Employment Income

- Minimum of 2 years of income history is required
- Most recent 1 month pay stub and most recent 2 years' W-2s
- Verification of Employment (VOE form, Form 1005) with breakdown of incomes

Seasonal Income

- Minimum of 2 years of income history is required
- Most recent 1 month pay stub and most recent 2 years' W-2s
- Verification of Employment (VOE form, Form 1005) with breakdown of incomes

Base Income Calculation

How Often Paid	How to Determine Monthly Income
Annually	Annual gross pay / 12 months
Monthly	Use monthly gross payment amount
Twice Monthly	Twice monthly gross pay x 2 pay periods
Biweekly	(Biweekly gross pay x 26 pay periods) / 12 months
Weekly	(Weekly gross pay x 52 pay periods) / 12 months
Hourly	(Hourly gross pay x average # of hours worked per week x 52 weeks) / 12 months

Verification of Income

Tax returns and W-2s

- Transcript of Tax Returns must be in file prior to closing (Form 4506-c is required)
- Verbal Verification of Employment must be done prior to closing

Rental Income

Documentations for Rental Income from Property **Other Than the Subject Property**

- Most recent 2 years signed tax return that includes Schedule 1 and Schedule E.
- Copies of the current lease agreement(s)

Calculating Monthly Qualifying Rental Income (or Loss)

If the borrower...	Then for qualifying purposes...
currently owns a principal residence (or has a current housing expense), and has at least 1 year history of documented property management experience	There is no restriction on the amount of rental income that can be used.
currently owns a principal residence (or has a current housing expense), and has less than 1 year history of documented property management experience	for a principal residence, rental income in an amount not exceeding PITIA of the subject property can be added to the borrower's gross income, or for an investment property, rental income can only be used to offset the PITIA of the subject property.
does not own a principal residence, and does not have a current housing expense	rental income from the subject property cannot be used.

Other Sources of Income

Documentation Requirements for Current Receipt of Income

- Most recent 1 month pay stubs and 2 years W-2s
- Canceled checks from the payer's account to the borrower
- Court records
- Copies of the borrower's bank statements showing the regular deposit of these funds

Alimony, Child Support, or Separate Maintenance

- Document that alimony, child support, or separate maintenance will continue to be paid for at least 3 years after the date of the mortgage application.
    - A copy of a divorce decree or separation agreement (if the divorce is not final) that indicates the monthly payment and states the amount of the award and the period of time over which it will be received.
- If a borrower who is separated does not have a separation agreement that specifies alimony or child support payments, payment amount can't be used.
- Check for limitations on the continuance of the payments, such as the age of the children for whom the support is being paid or the duration over which alimony is required to be paid.
- Document no less than 6 months of the borrower's most recent regular receipt of the full payment.
- Review the payment history to determine its suitability as stable qualifying income. To be considered stable income, full, regular, and timely payments must have been received for 6 months or

longer. Income received for less than 6 months is considered unstable and may not be used to qualify the borrower for the mortgage. In addition, if full or partial payments are made on an inconsistent or sporadic basis, the income is not acceptable for the purpose of qualifying the borrower.

Automobile Allowance

The borrower must have received payments for at least 2 years. Must add the full amount of the allowance to the borrower's monthly income and the full amount of the lease or financing expenditure to the borrower's monthly debt obligations.

Border Income

Border income is not an acceptable stable income.

Capital Gains Income

Capital Gains Income is generally a one-time transaction; therefore, it should not be considered as stable income.

Disability Income - Long Term

- Obtain a copy of the borrower's disability policy or benefits statement from the benefits payer to determine.
    - The borrower's current eligibility for the disability benefits.
    - The amount and frequency of the disability payments.
    - If there is a contractually established termination or modification date.
- Generally, long-term disability will not have a defined expiration date and must be expected to continue.
- The requirement for re-evaluation of benefits is not considered a defined expiration date.

- If a borrower is currently receiving short-term disability that will decrease to a lesser amount within next 3 years because they are being converted to long-term benefits, the amount of the long-term benefits must be used.

Employment Offers or Contracts

- Pay stub MIUST be obtained before funding
  - o Must obtain an executed copy of the borrower's offer or contract for future employment and anticipated income
- If pay stub can NOT be obtained before funding (Try to avoid this type of income)
  - o Following conditions MUST met
    - purchase transaction
    - principal residence
    - one unit property
    - the borrower is not employed by a family member or by an interested party to the transaction
    - the borrower is qualified using only fixed base income
  - o The employment offer or contract must
    - clearly identify the employer and the borrower, be signed by the employer, and be accepted and signed by the borrower
    - clearly identify the terms of employment, including position, type and rate of pay, and start date and non-contingent
- The borrower's start date must be no earlier than 30 days prior to the note date or no later than 90 days after the note date

- In addition to the amounts of reserves required by DU, one of the following is required
  - o 6 months PITIA reserves
  - o PITIA reserves for the number of months between the note date and the employment start date plus one.

Foster-Care Income

- Verify the income with letters of verification from the organizations providing the income
- Document that the borrower has a 2 year history of providing foster-care services. If the income was received for less than two years;
  - o the borrower has at least a 12 months history of providing foster-care services and
  - o the income does not represent more than 30% of the total gross income that is used to qualify for the mortgage loan

Interest and Dividends Income

If the borrower is keep buying and selling stocks, it is very hard to convince underwriter that income is stable. Try not to use this income.

- Documents a 2 years history of the income as verified by
  - o copies of the borrower's signed federal income tax returns or
  - o copies of account statements
  - o Average the income received for the most recent two years
  - o Subtract any assets used for down payment or closing costs

Non-occupant Borrower Income

A non-occupant borrower's income can be used as qualifying income for a principal residence with max 95% LTV.

Notes Receivable Income

- The income can be expected to continue for a minimum of 3 years from application date
- Must obtain a copy of the note(s)
- Document regular receipt of income for the most recent 12 months
- Payments on a note executed within the past 12 months may not be used as stable income

Retirement, Government Annuity, and Pension Income

- Document requirements
    - A statement from the organization providing the income
    - Award letter or benefit statement
    - A copy of financial or bank account statement showing regular deposits
    - a copy of signed federal income tax return
    - Most recent year's W-2 or 1099
- If retirement income is paid in the form of distribution from 401(k), IRA, or Keogh retirement account, determine whether the income is expected to continue for at least 3 years after the date of the mortgage application.
    - The borrower **must have unrestricted access to the accounts without penalty**

Royalty Payment Income

- Royalty contract, agreement, or statement confirming amount, frequency, and duration of the income
- Borrower's most recent year's signed tax return, including 1040, Schedule E

Schedule K-1 Income

- If the Schedule K-1 reflects distributions of income from the business, then no further documentation of access to the income or adequate business liquidity is required. The Schedule K-1 income may then be included in the borrower's income.
- If the Schedule K-1 does not reflect a documented, stable history of receiving cash distributions of income from the business, then you must confirm the business has adequate liquidity to support the withdrawal of earnings.
- If the borrower has a 2 year history of receiving "guaranteed payments to the partner" from a partnership or an LLC, these payments can be added to the borrower's income.

Social Security Income

Social Security income for retirement or long-term disability that the borrower is drawing from his or her own account/work record will not have a defined expiration date and must be expected to continue.

If Social Security benefits are being paid as a benefit for a family member of the benefit owner, that income may be used in qualifying if the remaining term is at least 3 years from the date of the mortgage application.

Asset

Document Requirements

- Bank statements must provide with all pages including blank pages if it has page numbers on it.
- Purchase: Most recent 2 months bank statements.

- Refinance: Most recent 2 months bank statements. Fannie Mae requires 1 month but there might be items on the bank statement that require explanation.
- Computer print-outs MUST show URL address at the bottom of the page

Depository Accounts

Funds held in a checking, savings, money market, certificate of deposit, or other depository accounts may be used for the down payment, closing costs, and reserves.

Unverified funds are not acceptable.

***All large deposits must be documented.**

Large Deposits: A single deposit that exceeds $1,000 or 50% of the total monthly qualifying income.

Business Assets

May be an acceptable source of funds for the down payment, closing costs, and reserves if

- Borrower has 100% ownership.
- Cash flow analysis to confirm that the withdrawal of funds will not have a negative impact on the business.

Gift Funds

Allowed for a principal residence or second home only.

Acceptable Donors

- A relative, defined as the borrower's spouse, child, or other dependent, or by any other individual who is related to the borrower by blood, marriage, adoption, or legal guardianship.
- a fiancé, fiancée, or domestic partner.

- If the borrower receives a gift from a relative or domestic partner who has lived with the borrower for the last 12 months, the gift is considered the borrower's own funds.

Minimum Borrower Contribution Requirements

- LTV, CLTV, HCLTV <= 80%: 100% gift is allowed.
- LTV, CLTV, HCLTV > 80%:
  - 1 unit: 100% gift is allowed.
  - 2 - 4 unit: 5% minimum borrower contribution from own funds required.

Documentation Requirements

- Gift letter from the donor with donor's information
- Verifying Donor's Ability
  - A copy of the donor's check and the borrower's deposit slip.
  - A copy of the donor's withdrawal slip and the borrower's deposit slip.
  - A settlement statement showing receipt of the donor's gift.
  - **If donor wires the funds to the closing agent, donor's ability is NOT required.**

Gift of Equity

- Allowed for principal residence and second home purchase transactions.
- Can be used fund all or part of the down payment and closing costs.
- **Cannot be used towards reserves.**
- Gift letter required.
- Settlement statement listing the gift of equity is required.

Interested Party Contributions (IPC)

Seller's contribution is considered as IPC. Sometimes listing, selling agents contribute to help to close the transaction.

Any IPC can only be used for non-recurring closing costs.

IPC Limits

Occupancy Type	LTV/CLTV Ratio	Maximum IPC
Principal residence or second home	Greater than 90%	3%
Principal residence or second home	75.01% – 90%	6%
Principal residence or second home	75% or less	9%
Investment property	All CLTV ratios	2%

Credit

Traditional Credit

- Inquiries: Must get LOE from the borrower for inquiries made past 120 days.
- Omitted Accounts: Supporting documentation is required.
- Judgments and Liens: Open judgments and all outstanding liens that are in the public records must be paid off at or prior to closing.
- Mortgage Delinquencies
  - Any reported 60 days late within the last 12 months are not ineligible.
  - Two or more lates in the last 12 months is not eligible.
- Past-Due, Collection, and Charge-Off of Non-Mortgage Accounts
  - Accounts that are reported as past due not reported as collection account must be brought current.

- **For 1 unit, principal residence properties, borrowers are not required to pay off outstanding collections or non-mortgage charge-offs-regardless of the amount.**
- For two-to-four units owner-occupied and second home properties, collections and non-mortgage charge-offs totaling more than $5,000 must be paid in full prior to or at closing.
- For investment properties, individual collection and non-mortgage charge-off accounts equal to or greater than $250 and accounts that total more than $1,000 must be paid in full prior to or at closing.

Non-traditional Credit

When borrower(s) doesn't have credit score due to no trade-lines, non-traditional credit can be used such as utility bills for most recent 12 months. When non-traditional credit is used, loan has to be manually underwritten.

Usable non-traditional credits

- Utilities, such as electricity, gas, water, etc.
- Medical insurance coverage excluding payroll deductions.
- Payments for household or renter's insurance.
- Payments to local stores, such as department stores, furniture stores, etc.
- Rental payments for durable goods, such as automobiles.
- Payment of medical bills.
- Payment of school tuition.
- Payments for child care.
- A loan obtained from an individual.

Credit Event Waiting Period

Events	Standard	Extenuating Circumstances
Bankruptcy Chapter 7 or Chapter 11	4 years from discharge or dismissal date	2 years from discharge or dismissal date
Bankruptcy Chapter 13	2 years from discharge date 4 years from dismissal date	2 years from discharge date
Multiple Bankruptcy within past seven years	5 years from most recent dismissal or discharge date	5 years from most recent dismissal or discharge date
Foreclosure	7 years	3 years 3 - 7 years restrictions • 90% max. LTV • Purchase, principal residence • Limited cash-out, all occupancy
Deed-in-Lieu Short sale	4 years	2 years

Monthly Debt Obligations

Alimony, Child Support, and Separate Maintenance Payments

If payments must continue to be made for more than 10 months, the payments must be considered as part of the borrower's recurring monthly debt obligations.

Bridge / Swing Loans

When a borrower obtains a bridge (or swing) loan, the funds from that loan can be used for closing on a new principal residence before the current residence is sold. This creates a contingent liability that must be considered part of the borrower›s recurring monthly debt obligations and included in the DTI ratio calculation.

Will not require the debt to be included in the DTI ratio if the following documentation is provided

- a fully executed sales contract for the current residence.
- confirmation that any financing contingencies have been cleared.

Business Debt in Borrower's Name

- Payment does not need to be considered as part of the borrower's DTI ratio if:
    - o If the account does not have a history of delinquency.
    - o If obligation was paid out of company funds (most recent 12 months of canceled company checks are required).
    - o Cash flow analysis of the business took payment of the obligation into consideration.
- Payment must be considered as debt payment if:
    - o If the business does not provide sufficient evidence that the obligation was paid out of company funds.
    - o If the account has a history of delinquency.

Court-Ordered Assignment of Debt

When a borrower has outstanding debt that was assigned to another party by court order such as under a divorce decree or separation agreement, it is not considered as borrower's debt.

Debts Paid by Others

- If 3rd party makes payment on an account, payment can be excluded from borrower's DTI calculation with evidence of most recent 12 months payment history by other party.
- Borrower's mortgage debt paid by 3rd party can be excluded if:
    - o The party making the payments is on mortgage note.

- o There are no delinquencies in the most recent 12 months.
- o The borrower is not using rental income from the property to qualify.

Deferred Installment Debt

- Must be included as part of the debt obligations.
  - o if the credit report does not show the payment amount, you must obtain copies of the borrower's payment letters or forbearance agreements for monthly payment amount.
- Deferred Student Loans:
  - o if the credit report does not show the payment amount, you must obtain copies of the agreement for the monthly payment amount or use 1% of the outstanding balance as monthly payment.

Federal Income Tax Installment Agreements

- When a borrower has entered into an installment agreement with the IRS, monthly payment must be considered as the borrower's monthly debt obligations.
- Must be paid off at or prior to closing, if there is any indication that a Notice of Federal Tax Lien has been recorded against the borrower in the county in which the subject property is located.
- Required documents
  - o An approved IRS installment agreement with the terms of repayment including the monthly payment amount and total amount due.
  - o Evidence that borrower is current on the payments and at least one payment must have been made prior to closing.

Garnishments

More than 10 months remaining must be included as debt obligations.

Home Equity Lines of Credit (HELOC)

Monthly payment must be included as debt obligation. If the payment is not required, you don't need to hit any amount as debt obligations.

Installment Debts

- consider as monthly debt obligation if there are more than 10 monthly payments remaining.
- a timeshare account should be treated as an installment debt even if reported as a mortgage loan.

Lease Payments

Lease payments must be considered as recurring debt obligations regardless of the number of months remaining.

Revolving Charge/Lines of Credit

If the credit report does not show a minimum payment amount, the lender must use a greater of $10 or 5% of the outstanding balance as the monthly debt obligations.

Debts Paid Off At or Prior to Closing

- Don›t include payment as monthly debt obligation if:
    - o Installment loans that are being paid off or paid down to 10 or fewer remaining monthly payments.
    - o If a revolving account balance is to be paid off at or prior to closing. - account does NOT need to be closed.

Collections, Charge-offs of Non-Mortgage Accounts, Judgments, and Liens

- Delinquent credit must be paid off at or prior to closing.
- Delinquent federal income taxes with monthly payment agreement must be paid in full at or prior to closing if there is any indication that a Notice of Federal Tax Lien has been recorded against the borrower.

Eligible Properties

1 to 4 unit properties only. Including SFR, Condo, PUD.

Condo and PUD project Review

Project Documentation

- Legal and recorded documents including the covenants, conditions and restrictions, declaration of condominium, or other similar documents that establish the legal structure of the project.
- Budgets, financial statements, and reserve studies.
- Construction plans.
- Architects' or engineers' reports.
- Completion reports.
- Project marketing plans.
- Environmental hazard reports.
- Attorney opinion.
- Appraisal reports.
- Evidence of insurance policies and related documentation.
- Condominium project questionnaires (Form 1076).

Project Review Methods

Project Type	Review Methods
Attached condo in a new or newly converted project	Full review
Attached condo in an established project	Based on the LTV, CLTV, and HLTV, occupancy, these projects may be used using a Limited review. None Limited Review projects must be reviewed using a: • Full review • FHA Project Approval (HUD review)
Unit in a new or established 2 to 4 unit condo project	Project review is waived
Detached unit in a new or established condo project	Project review is waived
Unit in a co-op project	Full review
Unit in a PUD project	Project review is waived
Unit in a condo project approved by the FHA	FHA Project Approval

Property types for Waiver of Project Review

- Detached condo units.
- 2 to 4 unit condo project.
- PUD project.
- Fannie Mae to Fannie Mae limited cash-out refinances with LTV < 80%.

Eligible for Limited Review

An attached unit in an established condo project

Occupancy	Max. LTV, CLTV, HCLTV
Principal residence	90%
Second home	75%
Investment property	75%

Project Full Review Requirements

- Processor does not need to review condo docs.
- No more than 15% of the total units may be 60 days or more past due.
- Budget review
    - Is adequate.
    - Provides for the funding of replacement reserves for capital expenditures and deferred maintenance that is at least 10% of the budget.
- Income excluded from the reserve calculation
    - incidental income for ongoing operations, maintenance, or capital improvements.
    - income collected for utilities.
    - income allocated to reserve accounts.
    - special assessment income.
- For investment property transaction in established projects at least 50% of the total units must be principal residence.

Additional Requirements for New and Newly Converted Condo Projects

- A certificate of occupancy (completion cert.) or other substantially similar document has been issued by the governmental agency.
- All the units and buildings in the legal phase are complete.
- At least 50% of the total units be under contract for sale to principal residence or second home purchasers.
- Individual units must be available for immediate occupancy at the time of loan closing.

Leasehold Estates

- The term of the leasehold estate must run for at least five years beyond the maturity date of the loan.
- The lease must provide that the leasehold can be assigned, transferred, mortgaged, and sublet an unlimited number of times either without restriction or on payment of a reasonable fee and delivery of reasonable documentation to the lessor.
- The lease must provide for the borrower to retain voting rights in any homeowners' association.
- The lease must not include any default provisions that could give rise to forfeiture or termination of the lease, except for nonpayment of the lease rents.
- The lease must provide lenders with
  - o the right to receive a minimum of 30 days' notice of any default by the borrower, and
  - o the option to either cure the default or take over the borrower's rights under the lease.

Accessory Dwelling Units (ADU)

- Only one ADU is permitted on the parcel of the primary 1 unit dwelling.
- ADUs are not permitted with a 2 to 4 unit dwelling.
- The ADU must
  - o be smaller in size to the primary dwelling.
  - o have the following separate features from the primary dwelling :
    - means of ingress/egress
    - kitchen

  - sleeping area
  - bathing area
  - bathroom facilities

- It is not considered an ADU if it can only be accessed through the primary dwelling or the area is open to the primary dwelling with no expectation of privacy.
- The kitchen must, at a minimum, contain the following:
  - cabinets
  - a countertop
  - a sink with running water
  - a stove or stove hookup
  - An independent second kitchen by itself does not constitute an ADU
  - The removal of a stove does not change the ADU classification.
- A borrower must qualify for the mortgage without considering any rental income from the ADU.
- ADU must be attached to a permanent foundation system in accordance with the manufacturer's requirements for anchoring, support, stability, and maintenance.
- Examples of ADUs
  - a living area over a garage
  - a living area in a basement
  - a small addition to the primary dwelling
  - a manufactured home
- ADU is legal if it is allowed under the current zoning code for the subject property.

Multiple Parcels

- Parcels must be adjoined to the other parcel.
- Exceptions:
    - o If the parcels are divided by a road
    - o If the parcel without a residence is a non-buildable lot (E.g. waterfront properties)
- Each parcel must have the same basic zoning.
- The entire property may contain only one dwelling unit.
- The mortgage must be a valid first lien that covers each parcel.

Mixed Use Properties

- The property must be a 1 unit dwelling that the borrower occupies as a principal residence.
- The borrower must be both the owner and the operator of the business.

Properties with Solar Panels

- Common ownership or financing structures:
    - o borrower owned panels
    - o leasing agreements
    - o separately financed solar panels where the panels serve as collateral for debt distinct from any existing mortgage
    - o power purchase agreements
- Properties with PACE loan are not eligible for delivery to Fannie Mae if the PACE loan is not paid in full prior to or at closing.

Appraisal Report

Appraisal Form Numbers

- 1004: SFRs, PUDs with interior and exterior inspections
- 1004 Desktop: SFRs, PUDs without interior and exterior inspections
- 1073: Condos with interior and exterior inspections
- 1025: 2- 4 unit properties with interior and exterior inspections
- 1004D: appraisal update and/or completion report

Age of Appraisal and Appraisal Update Requirements

- Within the 12 months prior to the date of the note and mortgage.
- When the effective date of the original appraisal report is more than 4 months but less than 12 months from the date of the note and mortgage, the appraiser must update the report with interior, exterior inspection and reviewing current market data.
- The appraisal update must occur within 4 months prior to the date of the note and mortgage.
- The original appraiser should complete the appraisal update.
- New Desktop appraisal is required if the original report is more than 4 months from the note and mortgage.

Use of an Appraisal for a Refinance Transaction

Applies to Fannie Mae direct lenders. Most mortgage lenders don't allow re-use of an original appraisal report.

Fannie Mae will allow the use of an original appraisal for used in purchase if the following requirements are met

- Rate & Term refinance only.
- The age of the appraisal report must be less than 12 months from the note date of the new transaction.

- If the appraisal report is greater than 4 months from the date of the note and mortgage, an appraisal update is required.
- The lender must ensure that the property has not undergone any significant remodeling, renovation, or deterioration.
- The borrower and the lender must be the same on the original and refinance transaction.

Accessory Dwelling Units (ADU)

- ADU is generally an additional living area independent of the primary dwelling that may have been added to, created within, or detached from the primary dwelling
- ADU must have basic requirements for living, sleeping, cooking, and bathroom facilities on the same parcel as the primary dwelling
- Living area of an ADU should not be included as Gross Living Area on the appraisal report
- If there's no permit, the appraiser must comment on the quality and appearance of the work and its impact, if any, on the market value of the subject property

Property Inspection Waiver (PIW)

If DU approves the loan with PIW eligible condition, appraisal report is not required

Insurance

Title Insurance

Title insurance must cover the loan amount

Property Insurance (Hazard Insurance)

The coverage must provide for claims to be settled on a replacement cost basis. Extended coverage must include, at a minimum, wind, hurricane, civil commotion (including riots), smoke, hail, and damages caused by aircraft, vehicle, or explosion

Fannie Mae does not accept property insurance policies that limit or exclude from coverage (in whole or in part) windstorm, hurricane, hail damages, or any other perils that normally are included under an extended coverage endorsement.

Additional requirements apply to properties with solar panels that are leased from or owned by a third party under a power purchase agreement or other similar arrangement.

For a first-lien mortgage secured by a property on which an individually held insurance policy is maintained, Fannie Mae requires coverage equal to the lesser of the following:

- 100% of the insurable value of the improvements, as established by the property insurer or;
- the unpaid principal balance of the mortgage, as long as it at least equals the minimum amount (80% of the insurable value of the improvements) required to compensate for damage or loss on a replacement cost basis. If it does not, then coverage that does provide the minimum required amount must be obtained.

Amount of Coverage

Insurance must cover 100% of the insurable replacement cost of the project improvements, including the individual units in the project. An insurance policy that includes any of the following coverage is acceptable

- Guaranteed Replacement Cost - the insurer agrees to replace the insurable property regardless of the cost.
- Extended Replacement Cost - the insurer agrees to pay more than the property's insurable replacement cost.
- Replacement Cost - the insurer agrees to pay up to 100% of the property's insurable replacement cost.

Name Insured

Coverage	Requirement for Named Insured
Condo projects	The policy must show the HOA as the named insured. **The "loss payable" clause should show the HOA or the insurance trustee as a trustee for each unit owner and the holder of each unit's loan.**
PUD	The policy must show the HOA as the named insured.

Mortgage Insurance (MI)

Borrower Paid vs Lender Paid

- Borrower Paid Plan: Borrower pays for the monthly MI
- Lender Paid Plan: Borrower pays one time MI fee to the lender and no monthly Mis

MI Coverage Requirements

Transaction Type	80.01 - 85.00% LTV	85.01 - 90.00% LTV	90.01 - 95.00% LTV	95.01 - 97.00% LTV
Fixed, term < 20 yrs	6%	12%	25%	35%
Fixed, term > 20 yrs	12%	25%	30%	35%
HomeReady Fixed, term < 20 yrs	6%	12%	25%	25%
HomeReady Fixed, term > 20 yrs	12%	25%	25%	25%

*MI requirements for HomeReady apply when HomeReady and HomeStyle Renovation are combined

Power of Attorney (POA)

Eligible Transactions

- Purchase
- Limited cash=out refinance

Documentation Requirements

- The lender obtains a copy of the POA
- The name(s) on the POA match the name(s) of the person on the relevant loan document
- The POA is dated such that it was valid at the time the relevant loan document was executed
- The POA is notarized
- The POA must reference the address of the subject property

Ineligible Agents

- Affiliate of lender
- Loan originator
- Affiliate of the loan originator
- Employee of the title insurance company
- Affiliate of the title insurance company or its employee
- Lender or employee of lender
- Property seller or any person related to the property seller, including a relative or affiliate
- Any real estate agent with a financial interest in the transaction or any person affiliated with such real estate agent

Made in the USA
Columbia, SC
11 May 2025

57788172R00065